P9-DDP-281

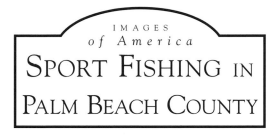

IMAGES
of America

SPORT FISHING IN
PALM BEACH COUNTY

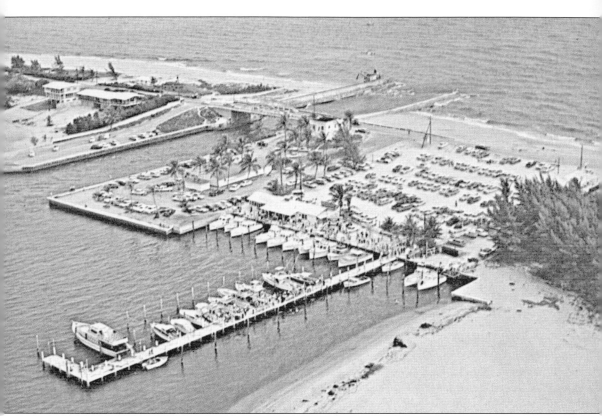

AERIAL VIEW. A bird's-eye view of the world famous Boynton Inlet shows the man-made channel as it was around 1960. Sea captains used great skill in maneuvering through the busy and treacherous inlet. (Courtesy Boynton Beach City Library Archives.)

FESTIVE DAY ON THE DOCKS. Miss America 1957, Marian McKnight, strolls down Lyman's Sport Fishing Docks. Miss America was in town to help Boynton Beach kick off the annual Boynton Beach Chamber of Commerce Fishing Tournament. (Courtesy Lyman family.)

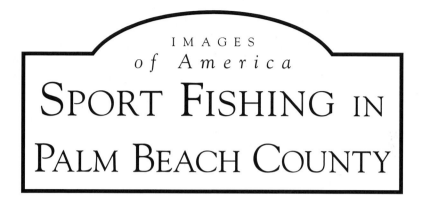

IMAGES
of America

SPORT FISHING IN
PALM BEACH COUNTY

Janet DeVries in conjunction with
the Boynton Beach City Library

ARCADIA
PUBLISHING

Copyright © 2008 by Janet DeVries in conjunction with the Boynton Beach City Library
ISBN 978-0-7385-5386-3

Published by Arcadia Publishing
Charleston SC, Chicago IL, Portsmouth NH, San Francisco CA

Printed in the United States of America

Library of Congress Catalog Card Number: 2007942669

For all general information contact Arcadia Publishing at:
Telephone 843-853-2070
Fax 843-853-0044
E-mail sales@arcadiapublishing.com
For customer service and orders:
Toll-Free 1-888-313-2665

Visit us on the Internet at www.arcadiapublishing.com

This book is dedicated to my two favorite anglers: my father, Frank Gardner, and my brother, Jimmy Gardner.

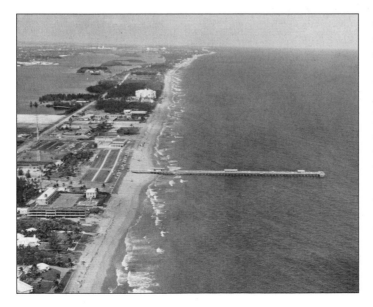

COASTAL PALM BEACH COUNTY. This aerial view of coastal Palm Beach County is from the 1960s. The view, looking north, shows the Atlantic Ocean on the right and the Lake Worth Lagoon, or Intracoastal Waterway, to the left. The William O. Lockhart Lake Worth Municipal Pier is in the center. Anglers can fish from jetties and piers or reef fish in 100 feet of water within a few minutes of leaving one of the four Palm Beach County inlets. (Photograph by Larry Witt; courtesy Grady Stearns.)

CONTENTS

ACKNOWLEDGMENTS

It all started with the charter boat captain Kenny Lyman. After he passed away in January 2007, his family, already familiar with Boynton Beach's Schoolhouse Children's Museum, inquired about adding a vignette concerning the area's deep fishing roots to the museum. A fund was set an educational exhibit about sport fishing history.

I attended Captain Kenny's memorial. Several dozen mates, captains, and friends shared stories about their fishing experiences. Each spoke of lessons learned on the docks, water, and wheelhouse. All this touched my heart, and I realized an important story was begging to be told. The fishing industry in Palm Beach County during the 1930s–1970s era was a key element, both economically and socially, in the growth of the county. Fishing was not only a sport; it was a way of life for many families in this coastal community.

It has been an honor and privilege to assemble a book celebrating the history of fishing in Palm Beach County. This historical tome was a combined effort of many people; I was merely the catalyst working to put the photographs, stories, and facts into one readable format. Cindy Lyman Jamison devoted countless hours setting up interviews and gathering photographs. Together we crisscrossed our way across the county, from Jupiter to Pompano. Steve Anton, photographer and videographer, recorded interviews and oral histories. The Boynton Beach City Library staff provided encouragement, research, and equipment for saving the images, recordings, and documents properly. John Jolley and Tom Twyford of the West Palm Beach Fishing Club (WPBFC) made the club's fishing archive available and gave great insight into the marine conservation efforts of the past, present, and future.

A myriad of interesting individuals provided valuable photographs or stories or otherwise helped to enrich this book. The fishing stories were brought to life via Shirley Adams, Jim Barry, Jim Branch, Bill Buckland, Joella Callaway, Angela Clark, Craig Clark, Dana Cook, Vern Pickup Crawford, Bob Davidoff, Anthony DiGiulian, Jean Dilcher, Jimmy Duncan, Paul Fasolo, Jeanette Garnsey, Susan Gillis, Gwen Hahn, Janet Hall, Greg Hertz, Bob Jamison, Laura Jervis, Dan Kleiser, Jeanie Lance, Howard Lawson, Jack Liggett, Allen Merritt, John and Marcia Miller, Alene and Vincent Molle, Charles Moore, Butch Moser, Beverly Mustaine, Marjorie Nelson, Michael Naughton, Dorothy Patterson, Geno and Karen Pratt, Sam Quincey, Linda Reeves, Kay Rybovich, Judy Sanders, John Schulz, Stan Sheets, Capt. Bouncer Smith, Nick Smith, Tim Smith, Grady Stearns, Barbara and Philip Traylor, Buddy Tuppen, Donald Van Epp, Anne Watts, and Jack Whittenborn.

INTRODUCTION

When historians review Florida's development, the role of inland or offshore fishing doesn't always get as much credit as it probably should unless it is about the Florida Keys or Apalachicola. A fairly recent publication on the history of Palm Beach County hardly mentions the vast fishing resources that have always been here and the significant roles they played attracting visitors and ultimately new residents. At the beginning of the 20th century, the quantity and quality of marine resources available to many area settlers was vital in sustaining their successful operations. As more arrived, utilization of these resources continued to increase. Throughout the 1920s and into the 1960s, city, county, and private businesses and individuals cooperatively began to realize and take advantage of this unique natural wealth. But today, in these more modern times, this relationship has become less well recognized, especially by those huge numbers of new residents with little or no historical perspective of the region who perhaps spent their lives in many of the country's big cities or at least had little experience with the ocean and its varying opportunities. The economic and social importance of fishing is further diminished by many newer organizations and activities competing for time and money, like the performing arts, professional sporting events, shopping malls, and other entertainment. All these things, combined with Florida's favorable climate, represent an attractive and highly diverse community of almost endless choices in business and leisure. What was once in the 1940s and 1950s the "in thing to do," like sailfishing, has now become just another one of many outdoor activities.

Palm Beach County's fishing heritage is one of the unique aspects of a community that gives the region character. It is a quality that makes this place so special to the people who call it home. It is refreshing when descendants of local pioneering families and their city government get together, as happened here, to try and rediscover some of the existing and valuable history and capture those moments in a way all generations can appreciate. Such is the case in this brief but well documented essay by Janet DeVries in cooperation with her colleague Cindy Lyman Jamison. They have endeavored diligently on a very skinny budget and short time frame to deliver a credible account about this area's fishing and some of its pioneering fishermen. The city of Boynton Beach and its library staff are also complimented for this effort and for developing a children's museum with depictions of early settlers and how commercial and recreational fishing became such an important part of the community.

For many years, Boynton Beach and much of Palm Beach County in general represented the "quiet life," with fishing and related social activities prominent but surrounded by agriculture and cattle or dairy farms. Everybody knew everybody else, or so it seemed. Hunting and fishing were major outlets for adults and youth. These activities, if successful—and they usually were—helped provide additional income and/or a cheap source of food for families and other area residents. Fish, spiny lobster, oysters, clams, crabs, doves, quail, hogs, deer, and rattlesnakes were plentiful.

Boynton Inlet (South Lake Worth Inlet), dug in 1926, and the plentiful nearby resources helped encourage local development at a time when growth was in its infancy. The earliest settlers are now gone, as are many later pioneers in fishing. Those who remain represent a vanishing breed that witnessed the resource at its greatest abundance and biodiversity at least up until the late 1960s. New generations, representing a shifting baseline, will never see it as it once was. Accounts by historians and the photographs are all that remain of days gone by.

Janet DeVries's pictures and narrative give a glimpse of that time before consequences of rapid development took place throughout South Florida. A burgeoning population stimulated the economy but at the expense of valuable productive habitat like sea grasses and mangroves, especially in the Lake Worth Lagoon.

Readers will appreciate Janet's stories of past captains and crews and clientele in the charter boat fishery and other private associations. This was a colorful group. They helped make social life in the Palm Beaches exciting. Catching a sailfish or a dolphin became routine with these guys and gals. Fittingly, their stories live on for generations while providing a baseline on how things used to be, an earlier era when life was less complicated and fishing took center stage.

—John W. Jolley
President of the West Palm Beach Fishing Club

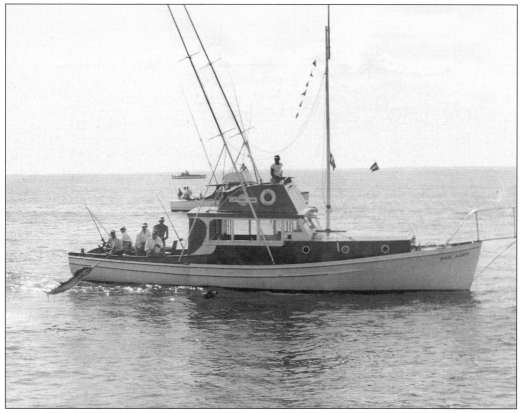

SILVER SAILFISH DERBY. Anglers participating in the West Palm Beach Fishing Club's annual Silver Sailfish Derby watch as another sailfish leaps from the water. The six red release pennants indicate that this was at least the seventh sailfish of the day. (Courtesy West Palm Beach Fishing Club [WPBFC].)

One

CHARTER BOATS
AND DRIFT BOATS

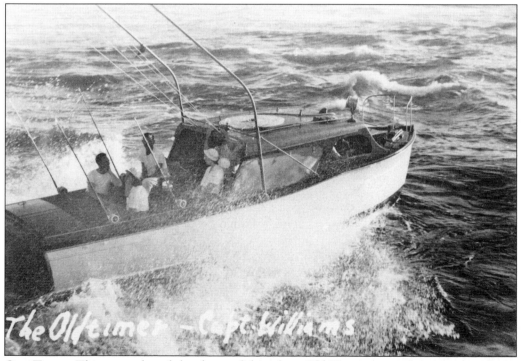

OLD TIMER. This party aboard the charter fishing boat *Old Timer* seems to be enjoying a day at sea. Notice there is no fly bridge or pulpit, as those designs came along later. Jack Williams, captain of the *Old Timer*, was originally a mechanic in the Glades. (Courtesy Jack Williams family.)

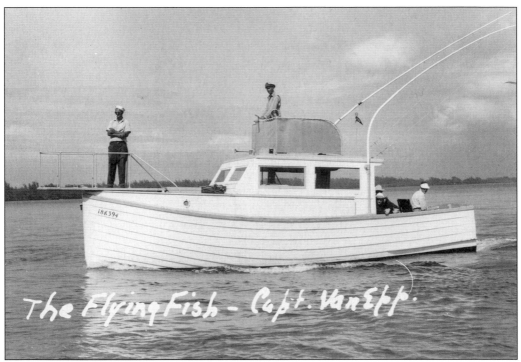

FLYING FISH. This is an early fishing boat with a lapstrake hull design. The lapstrake next to the keel was called the garboard strake. The ridges of the laps grip the water on the outside and stabilize the hull. After the 1920s, there was a revolution in boatbuilding, and people wanted smooth-hulled boats. The captain of the *Flying Fish* was Corwin Van Epp. (Courtesy Donald Van Epp.)

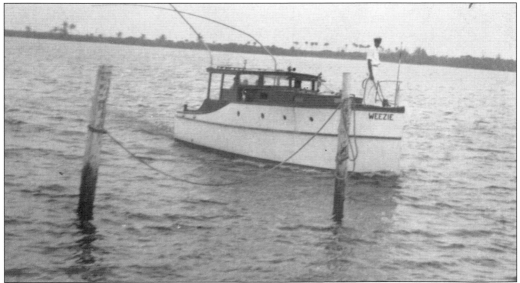

WEEZIE. Even before formal boat docks existed in the Boynton area, boats tied up near the Boynton Inlet. Capt. Harold Lyman stands on the bow of his first boat, *Weezie*. This early sport fishing vessel sported a simple design, with a harpoon pulpit, pilot cabin, Calcutta (cane pole) outriggers, and sleeping quarters. (Courtesy Capt. Jack Williams.)

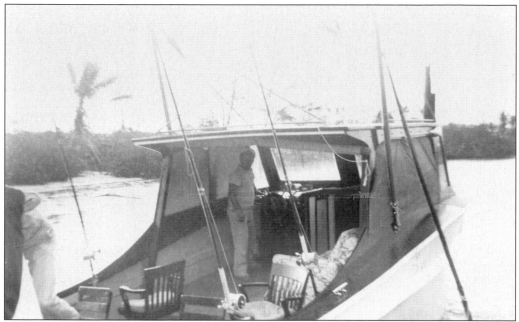

WEEZIE CABIN. Harold's father, Capt. Walter "Pop" Lyman, was the first commercial fisherman in south Palm Beach County and the first captain to navigate through the spillway now known as the Boynton Inlet after it was dug out in 1926. The back view of the *Weezie*, shown here in 1937, demonstrates the simple design and functionality of wooden fishing boats of the era. (Courtesy Lyman family.)

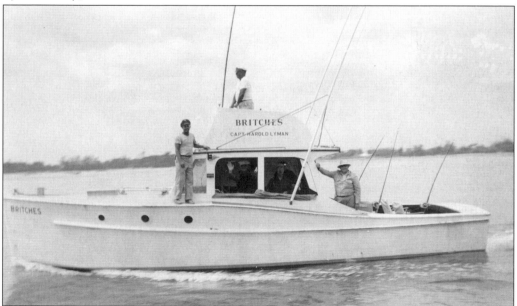

BRITCHES. While most of the present-day boat captains came to Boynton Beach because of the fine fishing, Capt. Harold Lyman had the good fortune of being born in Boynton. His father was the first commercial fisherman in this area, so naturally Harold became a fisherman too. Pictured here is his pride and joy, the *Britches*. It is fully equipped for offshore fishing, has twin 125-horsepower gasoline Chrysler engines for power, and is docked at Lyman's Docks. (Courtesy Lyman family.)

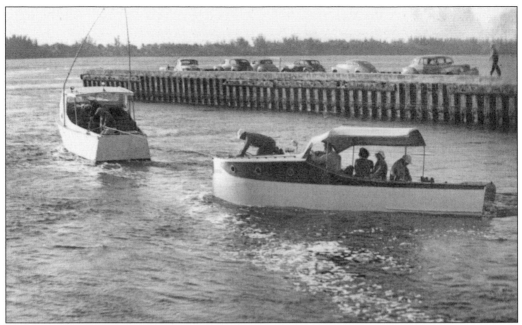

HELPING HAND. Capt. Jack Williams, piloting an unidentified boat, tows the *Lollipop* though the South Lake Worth (Boynton) Inlet. The *Lollipop* hit the jetty trying to navigate through the inlet into the ocean. This undated image is likely from the late 1930s. (Courtesy Capt. Jack Williams.)

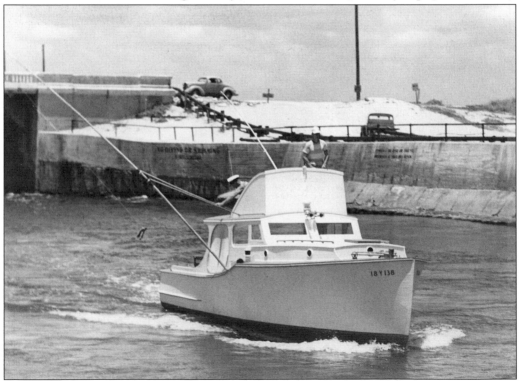

MANATEE. Capt. Howard Lawson secures the outriggers on his boat, the *Manatee*, as it motors through the Boynton Inlet in 1952. (Courtesy Howard Lawson.)

SEA BEE II. In the 1950s, the 42-foot wooden fishing yacht *Sea Bee II* was operated out of the Boynton Inlet Docks and later Lyman's Sport Fishing Dock and was captained by Harry "Cappy" Hager and later Butch Sylvester. This early photograph shows the boat with an umbrella on the flying bridge to provide shade in the days before the bimini top. (Courtesy Lyman family.)

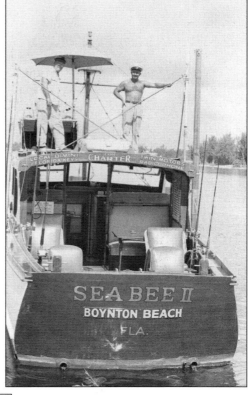

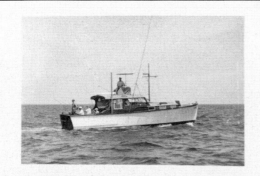

SPORT FISHING   REEF FISHING

Aboard 42-Foot Yacht SEA BEE II

Half Day or All Day
From the Boynton Inlet Docks

Fishing Trips to Bimini, Florida Keys
and Shark River

Cruising Any Place Any Time

Everything for Your Pleasure and Comfort

CAPTAIN HARRY HAGER

Phones: Delray Beach 5858: Boynton Beach 3201

SEA BEE ADVERTISEMENT. This ad for the *Sea Bee II* touts, "Fishing Trips to Bimini, Florida Keys and Shark River. Cruising Any Place Any Time Everything for Your Pleasure and Comfort." This design was likely produced by the Elco Boat Company. (Courtesy Dana Cook.)

13

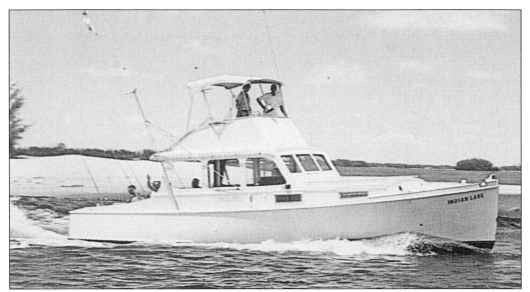

INDIAN LAKE. Born in 1919, Capt. Bill Keane was the popular skipper of the *Indian Lake*, a 42-foot fully equipped Matthews powered by twin 125-horsepower Chrysler engines. Known for his big catches and nicknamed Marlin Bill by Capt. Jack Smith, Keane often caught record marlin. Bill served in the navy in World War II and in 1954 was presented with a bronze plaque by the Coast Guard Auxiliary recognizing his valiant service for an ocean rescue. The *Indian Lake* docked at Boynton Inlet Docks. Captain Keane also ran the private boat *Enoch* for the Smith Brothers cough-drop heiress. (Courtesy Capt. Flip Traylor.)

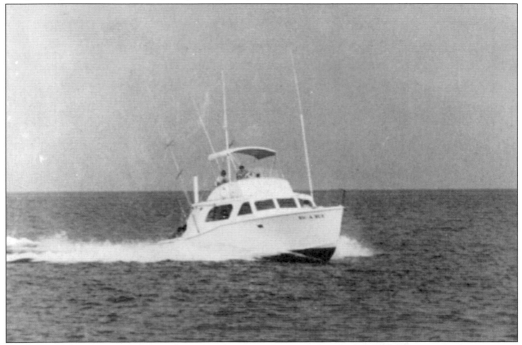

RICK A RUE. Capt. Fred Hastings ran the *Rick A Rue* out of Sailfish Marina. The boat was a Whiticar built in Stuart, Florida. Hastings, known as "Fearless Fred," was a fishing legend. Friends say he had a terrific sense of humor. (Courtesy Jim Duncan.)

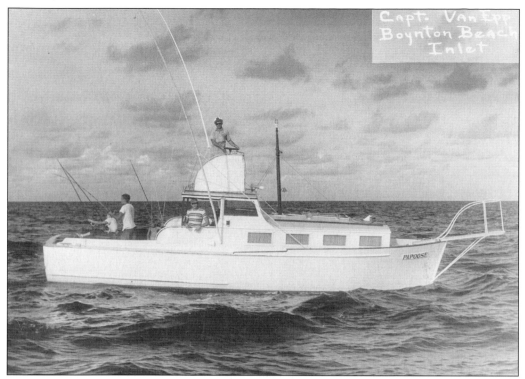

PAPOOSE. Capt. Corwin Van Epp motors the *Papoose* through the Boynton Inlet. The updated design included a harpoon pulpit, used for harpooning and assisting in landing an especially large fighting fish. (Courtesy Capt. Flip Traylor.)

MISS BEHAVIN. Capt. Charles "Red" Waggener's first boat was the *Twirp*. The *Miss Behavin*, shown here, was his second boat. Red was very well liked by his peers. His two sons, Ray and Wendell, also became charter boat captains. (Courtesy Capt. Flip Traylor.)

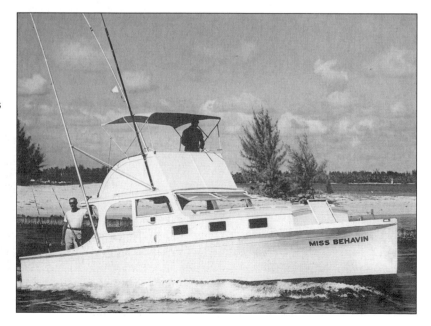

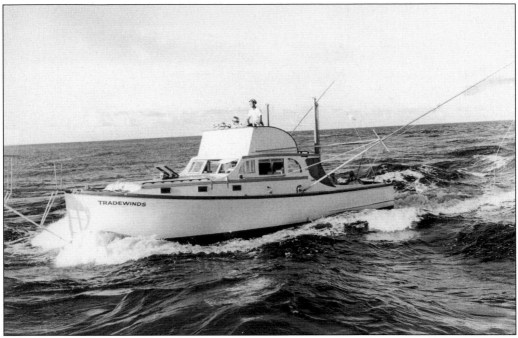

TRADEWINDS. The original *Tradewinds* was a 42-foot sport fisherman boat crafted by Adam Price. Capt. Harry Lawson, seen on the flying bridge, had his charter boat business from 1955 to 1959 and later switched to a drift boat. (Courtesy Howard Lawson.)

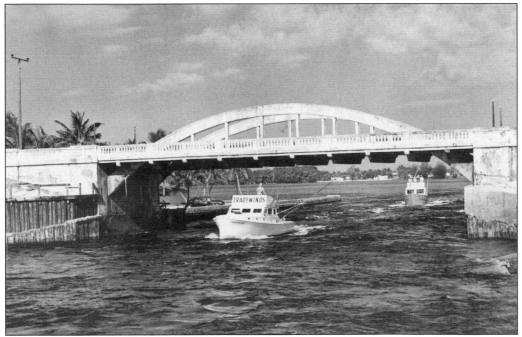

TRADEWINDS HEADS OUT TO SEA. It takes a skilled captain to navigate the Boynton Inlet. Capt. Harry Lawson, in the *Tradewinds*, heads out to sea. After a few years of running the *Tradewinds*, Captain Lawson decided drift boat fishing would be more profitable. (Courtesy Howard Lawson.)

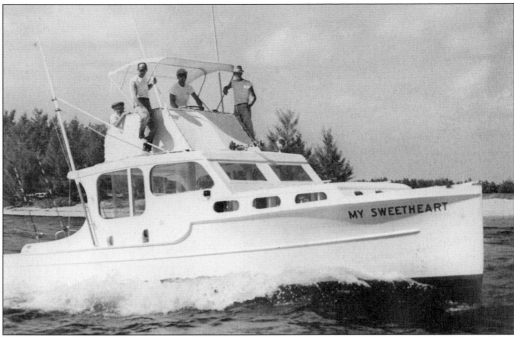

MY SWEETHEART. Capt. Homer Adams ran the charter fishing boat *My Sweetheart* starting in the 1940s. The *My Sweetheart* was a 48-foot boat built in Michigan. (Courtesy Capt. Flip Traylor.)

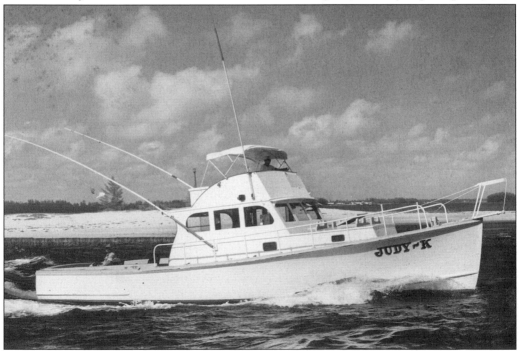

JUDY-K. The *Judy-K* was a 44-foot Downeaster built by Robert Rich in Southwest Harbor, Maine. It was a fully equipped diesel-powered sport fisherman boat. Verge (Nels) Nielson was the captain of the *Judy-K*, operating out of the Boynton Inlet Docks. Nels was born May 14, 1906, in Jutland, Denmark. (Courtesy Capt. Flip Traylor.)

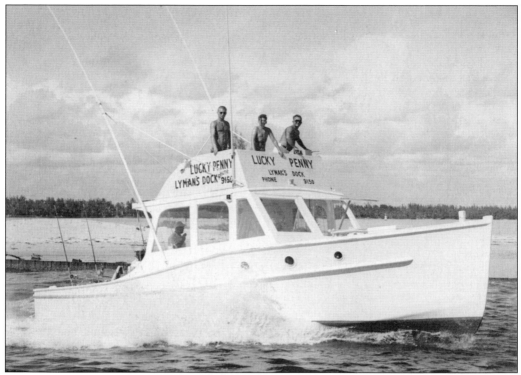

LUCKY PENNY. Capt. Kenny Lyman called all of his sport fishing boats the *Lucky Penny*. He named the boats after his wife, Helen "Penny" Powell. This boat was built up in Riviera Beach by Arlie Roberts. From left to right are mate Dick Greiner, now a local captain, Howard Lawson, and Capt. Kenny Lyman. (Courtesy Capt. Flip Traylor.)

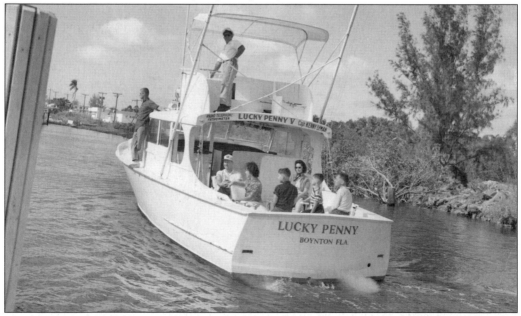

LUCKY PENNY V. Here is another of Captain Lyman's charter boats, named the *Lucky Penny V*. She was formerly the *Sea Bee*, now painted white. (Courtesy Lyman family.)

MISS CHEVY IV. In 1946, the world's first premier sport fishing boat, the 34-foot *Miss Chevy*, was designed by the Rybovich brothers and delivered to Charles Johnson. In 1947, the second Rybovich was delivered to Tony "Big Tuna" Accardo, the heir apparent to Al Capone's empire. In 1951, Charles Johnson commissioned his second Rybovich, the *Miss Chevy IV*. Shown here, it is the first sport fishing boat with an aluminum tuna tower, raised foredeck, and broken sheer line. (Courtesy WPBFC.)

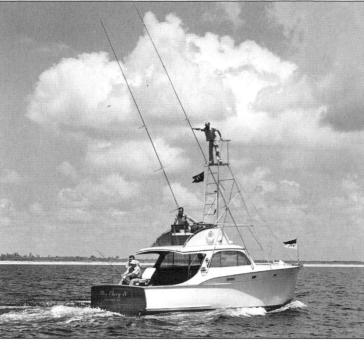

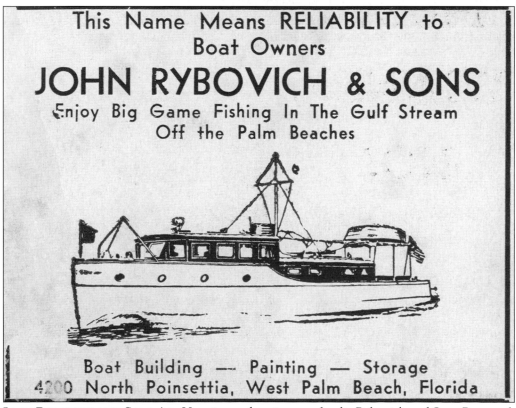

This Name Means RELIABILITY to
Boat Owners

JOHN RYBOVICH & SONS

Enjoy Big Game Fishing In The Gulf Stream
Off the Palm Beaches

Boat Building — Painting — Storage
4200 North Poinsettia, West Palm Beach, Florida

JOHN RYBOVICH AND SONS AD. Here is an advertisement for the Rybovich and Sons Boatyard. Rybovich boats are still highly sought after today. (Courtesy Jimmy Duncan.)

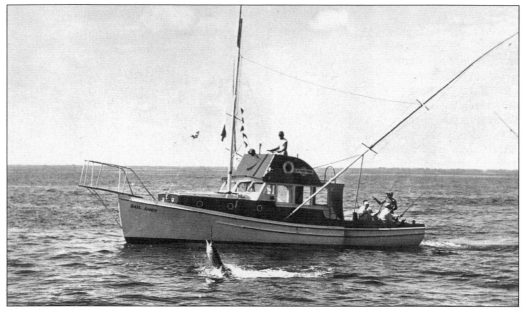

SAIL AHOY. This was the original *Sail Ahoy*. The later and most famous version was a Rybovich, the original *Miss Chevy*. The boat was brought down from New Jersey. Capt. Frank Ardine is pictured on the flying bridge. Notice the leaping sailfish. (Courtesy WPBFC.)

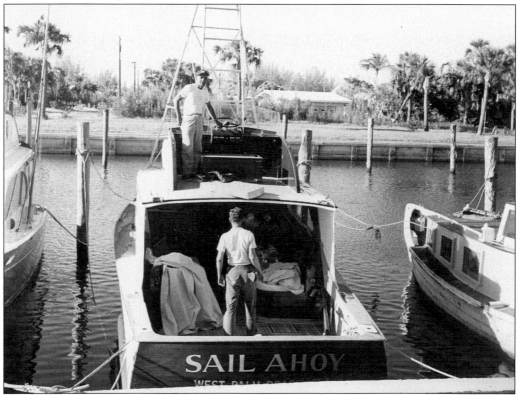

INTERIOR VIEW OF SAIL AHOY. The interior of the *Sail Ahoy* is seen here docked up. This later version of the *Sail Ahoy* was built by John Rybovich and sons. (Courtesy WPBFC.)

SAIL AHOY IN LAKE WORTH LAGOON. Many people say the radical sheer line and first-ever aluminum tuna tower of this Rybovich-built boat commanded the attention of the sport fishing community. The *Miss Chevy IV* was one of the first large boats made of planked mahogany. The Rybovich Brothers were among the first to experiment with fiberglass and epoxy resins, turbine engines, and other technologies. (Courtesy WPBFC.)

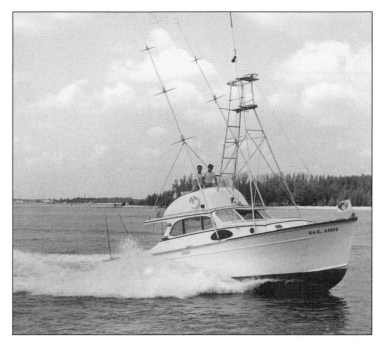

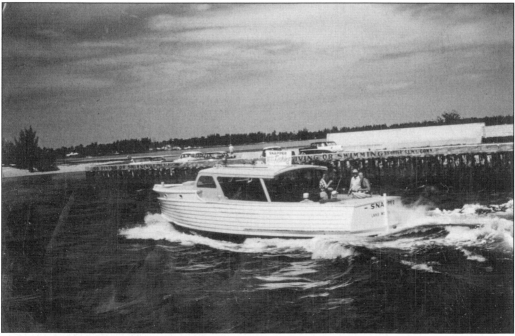

SNAPPER. This drift fishing boat was called the *Snapper*. This party boat with the lapstrake-hull design made daily trips into the Gulf Stream, where anglers experienced bottom reef fishing. The name of the boat, *Snapper*, and the name of the city, Lake Worth, Florida, are painted on the stern. (Courtesy Capt. Tim Smith.)

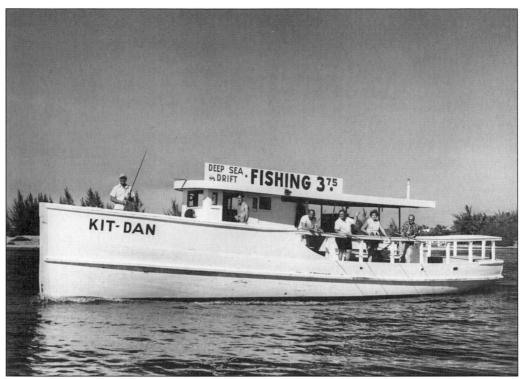

KIT-DAN. This boat was a converted 50-foot diesel-powered navy liberty launch. Capt. Harry Lawson built a wheelhouse and made other conversions. Here anglers can be seen enjoying a day of drift boat fishing. (Courtesy Howard Lawson.)

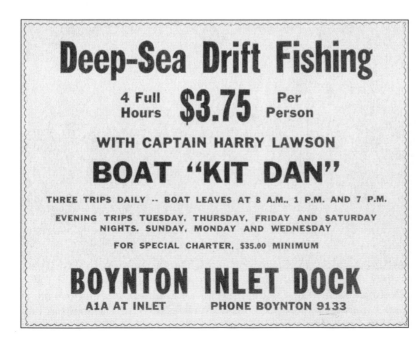

Deep-Sea Drift Fishing

4 Full Hours **$3.75** Per Person

WITH CAPTAIN HARRY LAWSON

BOAT "KIT DAN"

THREE TRIPS DAILY -- BOAT LEAVES AT 8 A.M., 1 P.M. AND 7 P.M.

EVENING TRIPS TUESDAY, THURSDAY, FRIDAY AND SATURDAY NIGHTS. SUNDAY, MONDAY AND WEDNESDAY

FOR SPECIAL CHARTER, $35.00 MINIMUM

BOYNTON INLET DOCK

A1A AT INLET   PHONE BOYNTON 9133

AD FOR *KIT-DAN.* This 1950s advertisement for deep-sea drift fishing excursions aboard the *Kit-Dan* with Capt. Harry Lawson shows the fee for a four-hour trip at $3.75 a person. The boat was always in use during the winter season, which was October to May, and made three trips per day offshore. (Courtesy Howard Lawson.)

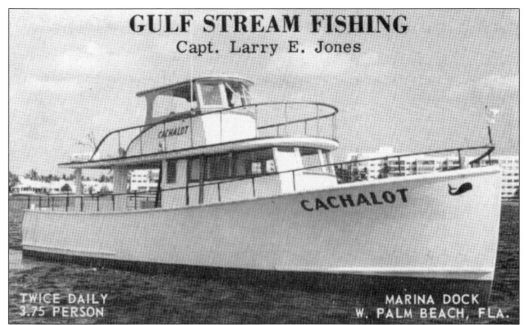

GULF STREAM FISHING
Capt. Larry E. Jones

CACHALOT

TWICE DAILY
3.75 PERSON

MARINA DOCK
W. PALM BEACH, FLA.

CACHALOT. In the 1950s, a half-day drift fishing trip aboard Capt. Larry E. Jones's *Cachalot* cost $3.75. The boat left from the West Palm Beach Marina dock twice a day. The boat was also available for special night fishing excursions. It was a family business operated by Larry Jones and his son. (Courtesy Capt. Tim Smith.)

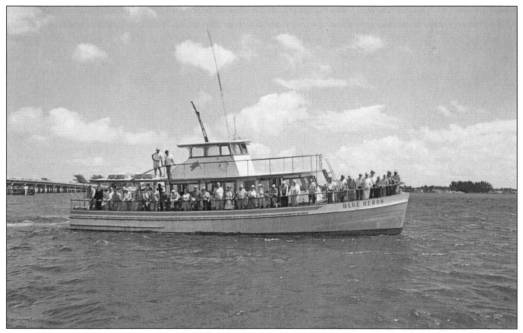

BLUE HERON DRIFT FISHING. This ocean fishing party boat was owned and operated by Blue Heron Docks in Riviera Beach near the Singer Island Bridge. The 65-foot boat with three diesel engines boasted, "Radio, phone, and fish finder, clean rest rooms for your comfort, pleasure and safety." Harry Miggle owned the Blue Heron fleet. (Courtesy Capt. Tim Smith.)

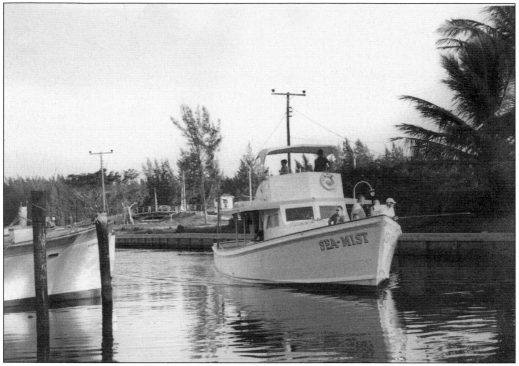

SEA-MIST. When the *Sea-Mist*, owned by the Garnsey-Hall family, first came down south, it parked at Lyman's Docks. Later the family bought the Boynton Beach Marina from Duncan Hunter and renamed it the Sea Mist Marina. In this photograph, Capt. Wendall Hall drives the *Sea-Mist* back to its dock at the Boynton Marina and mate Jim Ross, with the gaff, is ready to grab the lines. (Courtesy Garnsey family.)

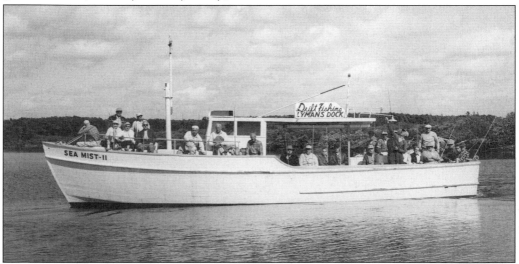

SEA-MIST II. The *Sea Mist II* was the name of the boat when the Halls bought it. The boat in the top photograph, the *Sea Mist*, is actually newer than the one in this photograph. This vessel was a popular drift fishing boat owned and captained by Wendall and Janet Hall. In 1960, Hall was the only licensed woman captain operating in this area, having obtained her captain's license in 1934. (Courtesy Boynton Beach City Library Archives.)

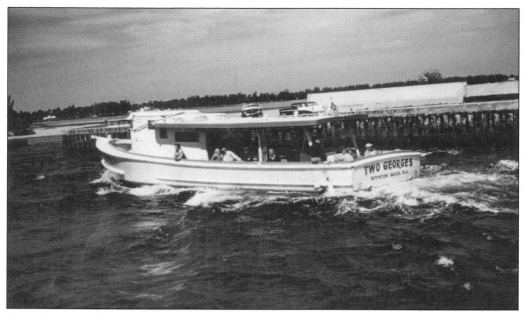

TWO GEORGES. The drift boat *Two Georges* glides into the South Lake Worth (Boynton) Inlet. For many years, the head boat was owned by George and Lori Culver. The vessel was 60 feet long with twin diesel motors, and the original fare to come aboard was $4.75. In 1962, the *Two Georges* tragically capsized in heavy ground seas (big, long waves that come in from far out at sea), and five people were killed. Today a popular restaurant called Two Georges is nestled along the Intracoastal Waterway in Boynton Beach and has a dock for diners who arrive via boat. (Courtesy Boynton Beach City Library Archives.)

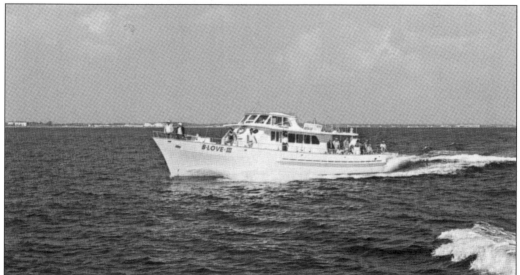

B-LOVE III. Captained by Alan Lebrun, *B-Love III* was docked at the Lantana Sportsman Park Docks. The *B-Love III* was a Lydia boat built in Stuart. It was originally crafted to be a yacht, but the man who commissioned it went bankrupt. With 77 feet of double-planked mahogany, the *B-Love* was the Cadillac of drift boats. The vessel was named after the owner's daughter, Barbara. Today the *Lady-K*, a 70-foot fiberglass Bonner boat, has replaced the *B-Love* at the docks at the Lantana Sportsman Park Docks. (Courtesy Capt. Tim Smith.)

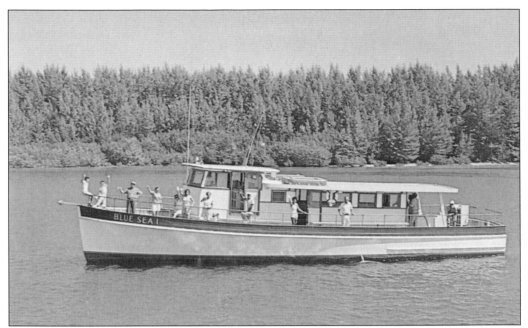

BLUE SEA I. Passengers on Capt. Ted Brower's *Blue Sea I* wave for the camera in this 1950s postcard image. The drift boat took anglers reef fishing twice a day and was docked at Riviera City Docks. The back of the card bears this advertisement: "Featuring the finest drift fishing—65 ft.—Three Diesels—U.S. Coast Guard approved—Ship to Shore Radio—Depth Recorder—All the latest tackle." (Courtesy Capt. Tim Smith.)

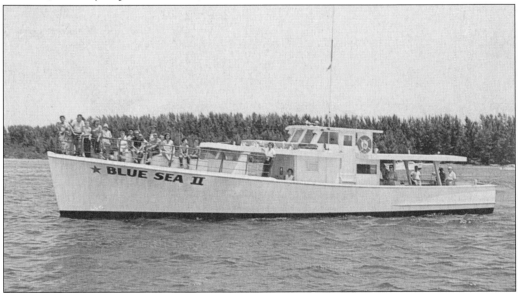

BLUE SEA II. A large group of anglers gather at the bow of the *Blue Sea II*. The photograph is from a postcard advertising Capt. Ted Brower's *Blue Sea II* out of the Riviera City Docks. The card also boasts, "Filled with thrills—Packed with excitement." The Blue Sea fleet was originally docked at old Layton's trailer park before moving to the city marina in Riviera Beach. Captain Brower was the first to have a drift boat in the north end of Palm Beach County. (Courtesy Capt. Tim Smith.)

Two

HOOK 'EM EARLY

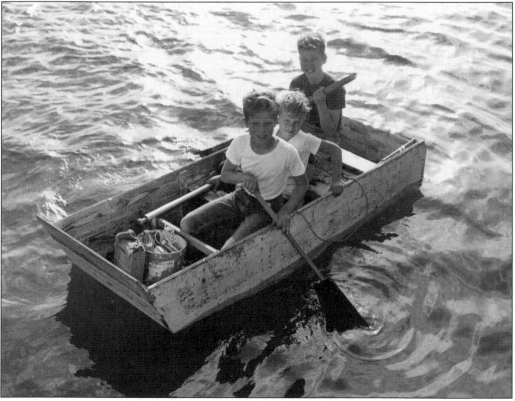

HOMEMADE FUN. Many Palm Beach County youngsters fished from small skiffs or homemade boats such as this one in the 1940s, 1950s, and 1960s. These three unidentified children are obviously enjoying a day of smooth seas in this tiny craft. (Courtesy WPBFC.)

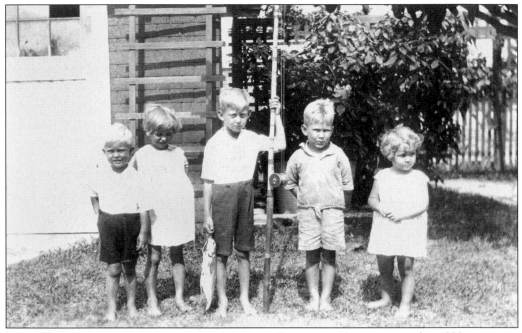

POMPANO. Youngsters in this 1929 photograph show off the first pompano caught by Bob Miller of Delray Beach. Pictured from left to right are John Miller, Norma Miller Brown, Bob Miller, Johnny Thieme, and Dorothy Thieme. Since this was during the Great Depression, the fresh fish was probably going to be pan-broiled in bacon fat, adding some much-needed protein to their pioneer diets. (Courtesy John and Marcia Miller.)

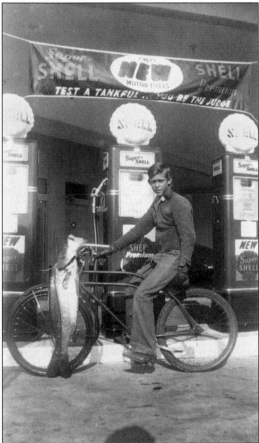

TO MARKET. John "Dude" Miller of Delray is pictured with one of three snook he caught under the Delray Bridge in 1938. This fish weighed 25 pounds. John pedaled his bike to Billings Fish Market on Atlantic Avenue and Fifth Avenue to sell the fish for 10¢ a pound. It took him three trips on his bicycle, but he made $7.60 in one day in January 1938. Unlike back then, snook today are game fish and illegal to sell. (Courtesy John and Marcia Miller.)

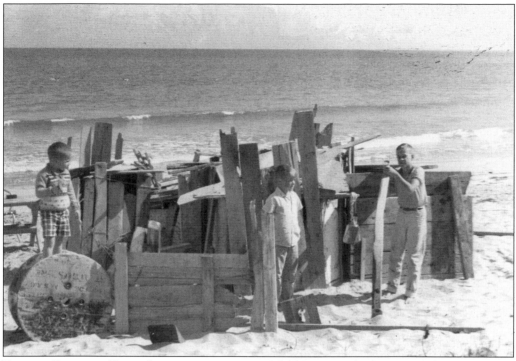

FISHING SHELTER. Shown here in 1963, from left to right, are Casey Shea, Danny Shea, and Douglas Bournique. As youngsters, the kids spent their days along the waterfront in Palm Beach, fishing and building forts from driftwood and other items that floated in. Seen to the right is a flexible bar that was a spring to launch water balloons. Both Shea brothers became sea-faring boat captains. (Courtesy Capt. Danny Shea.)

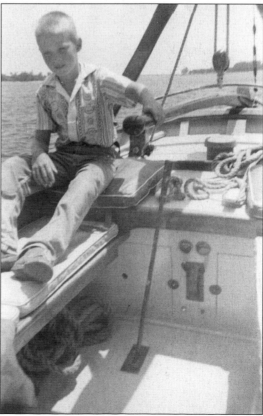

AT THE HELM. Ten-year-old Danny Shea was already comfortable piloting this fishing boat along the Intracoastal Waterway in this 1961 photograph. He learned about fishing and boating from local captains, becoming skilled in everything from shining the hardware and changing the oil to painting and fixing the head. His dad was a sailor and would drop him off at the docks after school. He learned to navigate with just a compass and a watch in the days before GPS. (Courtesy Capt. Danny Shea.)

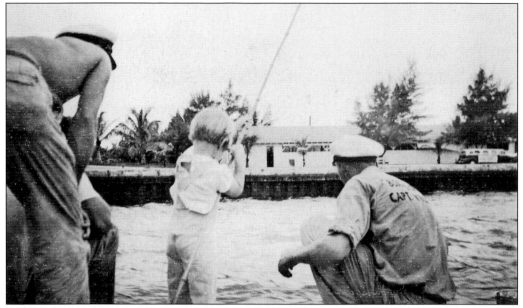

GOGGLE-EYES. Fishing off the Boynton Inlet wall in the 1940s, little Marie Williams tries her hand with the reel. With instruction and encouragement from her father, Capt. Jack Williams, Marie caught several goggle-eyes, a kind of fish used as bait and also called a big-eyed scad. (Courtesy family of Capt. Jack Williams.)

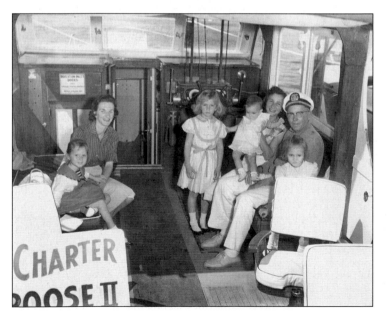

VISITING DAD. Capt. Corwin Van Epp and his wife, Gigi (right), smile for this 1957 photograph taken aboard his charter fishing boat the *Papoose II*. Three of their children are with them on the right. The Van Epp family is joined by Shirley Adams (wife of Capt. Homer Adams) and daughter Marcy (left). The captains' wives and children would often go down to the dock at 5:00 p.m. to watch the boats return. (Courtesy Shirley Adams.)

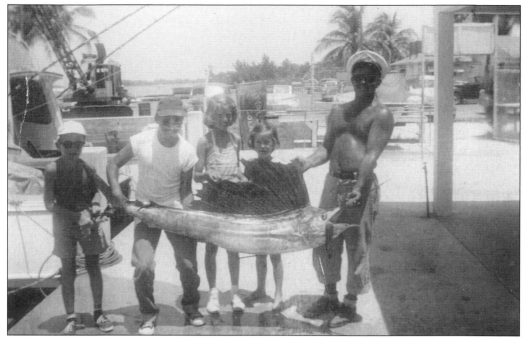

SAILFISH SMILES. This group of children is all smiles after catching a sailfish aboard the *Lucky Penny*. Capt. Kenny Lyman (right) holds the bill and dorsal fin while Sherman "Buddy" Tuppen (second from left) grasps the tail of the fish. When hooked, a sailfish will leap, twist, and tail-walk on the water in a struggle to break loose. Captain Lyman delighted in helping youngsters learn to fish. (Courtesy Buddy Tuppen.)

STRING OF FISH.
Young Buddy Tuppen
displays a string of
trout and snook he
caught just south
of Lantana Boat
Yard in 1952. Bud
grew up helping in
the family store,
Tuppen's Marine,
in Lake Worth and
fishing. (Courtesy
Bud Tuppen.)

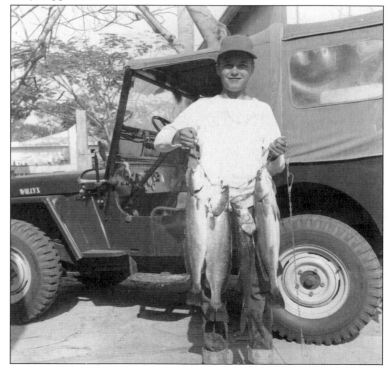

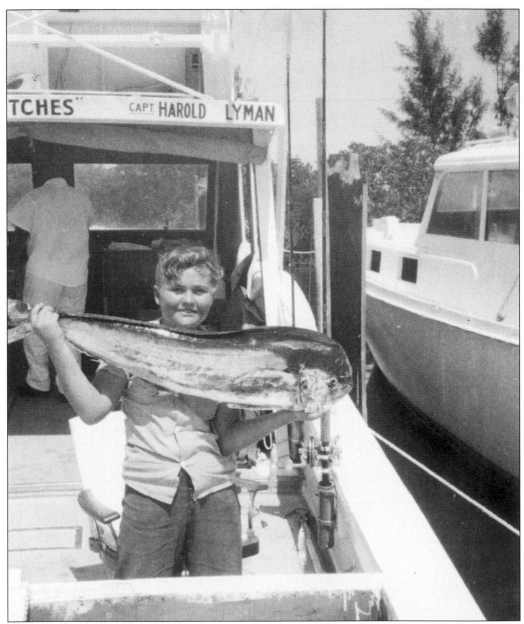

BUTCH MOSER. Ten-year-old Butch Moser displays an Atlantic dolphin he caught on Capt. Harold Lyman's sport fishing boat, the *Britches*, in the late 1950s. Butch learned more from the local boat captains than he did from formal schooling. After years of washing boats, selling fish, and serving as first mate, Butch knew he wanted to make a career out of fishing. These days, he serves as a guide on Lake Ida in Delray Beach, helping anglers land largemouth and peacock bass. (Courtesy Butch Moser.)

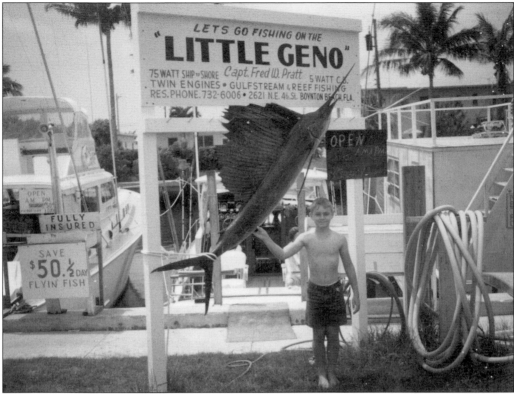

LITTLE GENO. The namesake for a series of fine sport fishing boats docked originally at Boynton and then at Lantana Sportsman Park Marina, young Geno Pratt grins while touching a mighty sailfish caught aboard the charter boat owned by his father, Capt. Fred Pratt. The original *Little Geno* was first launched in 1961 and boasted twin engines and 75-watt ship-to-shore and 5-watt citizen's band radios. (Courtesy Capt. Geno Pratt.)

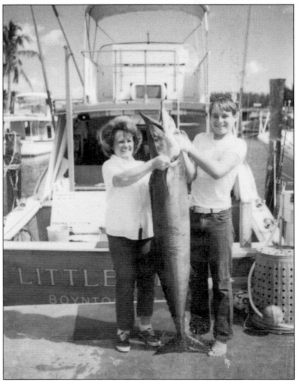

NOT-SO-LITTLE GENO. This late-1960s snapshot shows that Geno Pratt has grown up some and is taller than his mother, Mae. It takes the two of them to hold up the enormous kingfish, which is larger than Mrs. Pratt. (Courtesy Capt. Geno Pratt.)

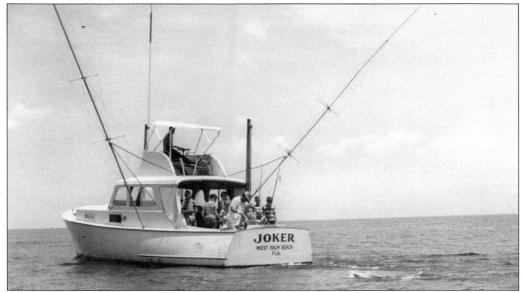

BEV SMITH FORD AND KRUISE KIDS PROGRAM. Bev Smith, a Ford automobile dealership owner, moved to Florida with his family in 1953. He fostered an exciting marketing plan designed to introduce children to the sport of fishing. Local children entered a drawing in the showroom, and each week six lucky children between the ages of 7 and 12 were selected to participate in a half-day ocean fishing trip. From 1957 to 1965, hundreds of children fished from Smith's boat *Tranquil*. Each year, a big Kruise Kids Jamboree was held at Bill's Marina, and local charter boats would join forces to give more kids a special day. The two photographs shown here are from an early 1960s Kruise Kids Jamboree. (Courtesy Vern Pickup Crawford and Nick Smith.)

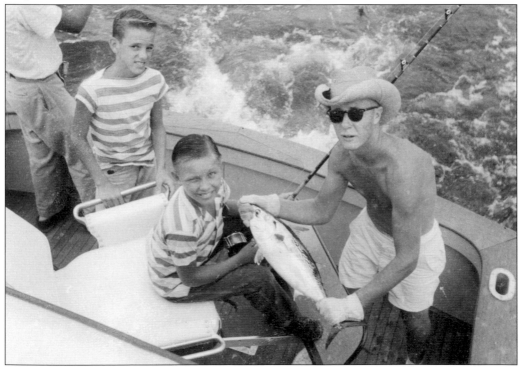

CAPT. ALAN LEBRUN. This group of 11- or 12-year-old boys did some work fixing up the *Lucky Penny V* when Capt. Kenny Lyman first bought it. After the work was complete, Kenny took them all on their first fishing trip. Alan Lebrun is the fourth boy from the left. His day of fishing led to a lifetime involved in the sport. Alan became Captain Alan and runs the *Lady-K* of the B-Love Fleet at Lantana Sportsman Docks. (Courtesy Lyman family.)

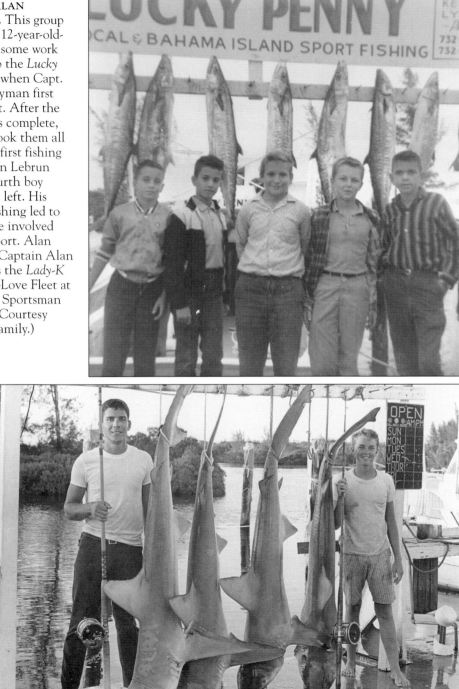

SHARK FISHING. Alan Lebrun (right) and friend Lynn Woofter display four sharks they caught while fishing. The image is from the 1970s, when shark fishing was a popular sport. (Courtesy Lyman family.)

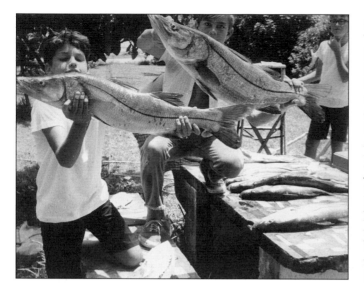

CAUGHT IN THE CANAL. Taken at the C-15 Canal (known by locals as the old Boynton spillway), this 1964 image captures the fun and adventure of the day, as cousins Paul Fasolo and Pat Plenzio hold up some snook. As youngsters, the Fasolo boys would wait until their dad, Joe, came home and drove them down to the Boynton Inlet to see what the boats had caught. They would marvel at the abundance of blue claw crabs and swamp rabbits in the vicinity. (Courtesy Paul Fasolo.)

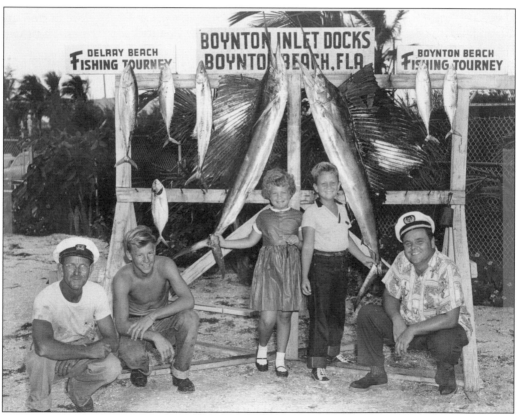

TWIN SAILS. A happy girl and a smiling boy each grasp a tail of sailfish caught in the Boynton Beach/Delray Beach Fishing Tourney. Capt. Harry Lawson is on the left, mate Jimmy Lawson is in the center, and Capt. Angelo Phillips is on the right. Captain Lawson was sometimes affectionately called Popeye. (Courtesy Howard Lawson.)

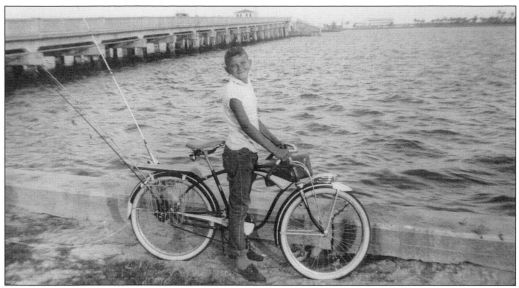

LOVES TO FISH. Jimmy Duncan rode his bicycle equipped with not one but two fishing poles to the Palm Beach Pier. Many kids who grew up in Palm Beach County did the same thing. Kids who spent lots of time on the fishing piers were called pier rats. It was a great place to grow up, and today many pier rats have become some of Palm Beach County's best citizens. (Courtesy Capt. Jim Duncan.)

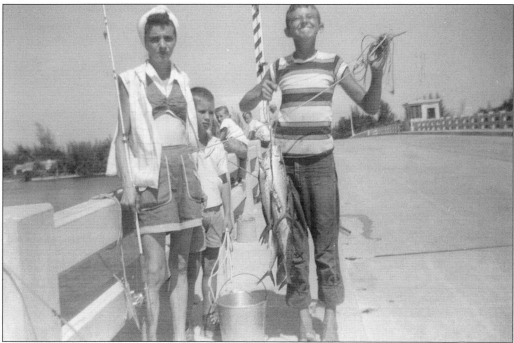

BEAMING FISHERMAN. Jimmy Duncan (right) bursts with pride as he stands on the Palm Beach Pier holding up numerous Spanish mackerel he caught. Jimmy's mother (left) often took the kids fishing on the pier. Jimmy's brother is the boy holding a rope. Other boys look on in the background. Jimmy grew up to be a charter boat captain and now collects old fishing tackle. (Courtesy Capt. Jim Duncan.)

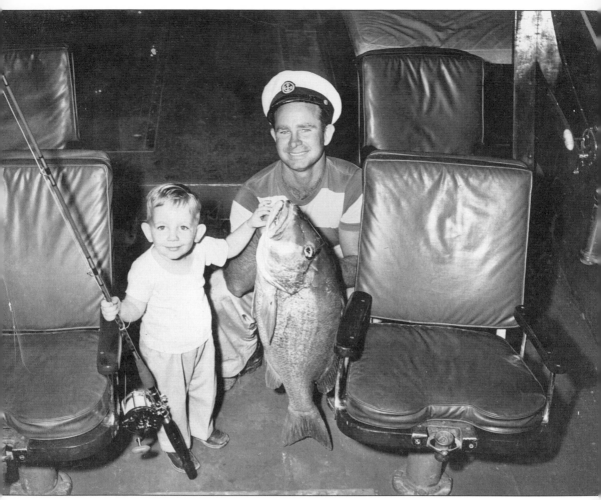

SON OF A SAILOR. Capt. Kenny Lyman and his two-year-old son, Walter "Skip" Lyman, pose in this 1949 image with a large snapper. Walter was named after his grandfather, one of this area's first commercial fishing captains. This fishing family used the photograph for their 1949 Christmas card. (Courtesy Lyman family.)

Three

REEL WOMEN FISH

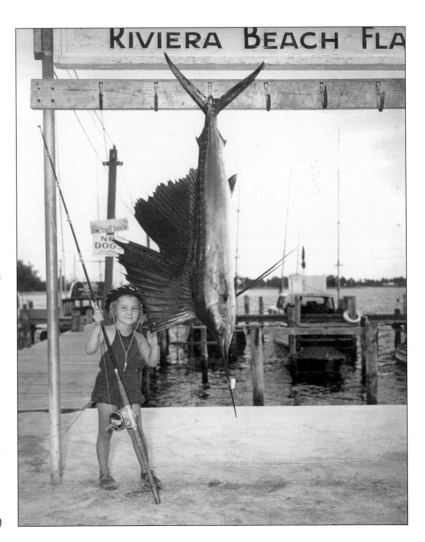

PROUD LITTLE LADY. Most women anglers are warmly welcomed into sport fishing. Many captains claim that the ladies often bring them luck. In the last 60 years, women have proven their skill landing big game fish. This young angler gets up close and personal with a large sailfish she presumably caught with her big rod. (Courtesy WPBFC.)

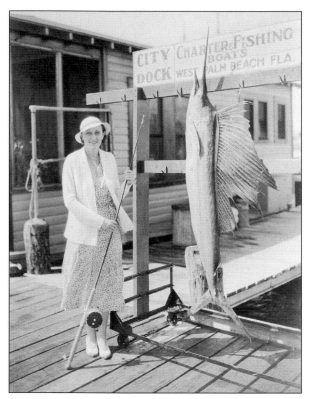

EARLY FEMALE ANGLERS. These Palm Beach County photographs are from the early 1930s. In each, an unidentified lady poses with a sailfish while holding a fishing rod. A sign reads "City Charter Fishing Boats Dock, West Palm Beach, Fla." in the image to the left. Women have made great advancements in the sport of fishing and many ladies hold international records. (Courtesy WPBFC.)

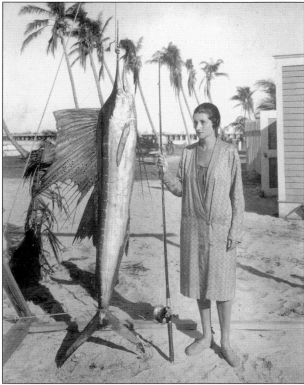

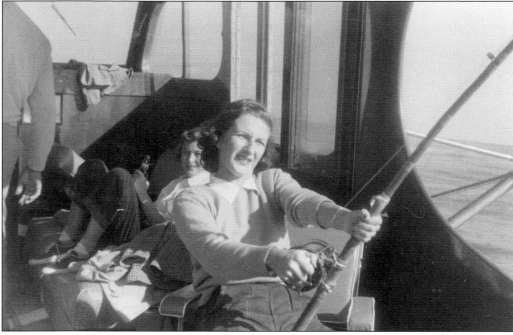

MISS SHIRLEY. Twenty-year-old Shirley Metcalf is shown in the fighting chair aboard *My Sweetheart* with Capt. Homer Adams. Shirley, who had recently moved to Delray Beach from Grand Rapids, Michigan, was on one of her first dates with Captain Adams. After hooking that beautiful sailfish, which Captain Adams promptly released, Shirley took a liking to big game fishing and married Captain Adams. (Courtesy Shirley Adams.)

BARBARA SPINKS TRAYLOR. Traylor, wife of Capt. Philip "Flip" Traylor, shows off a sailfish she caught in a 1970s tournament in Walker's Cay, Bahamas. Capt. Flip Traylor grew up fishing the waters of Palm Beach County and beyond in his many years as a private captain. Today he is also a commercial fisherman. (Courtesy Capt. Flip Traylor.)

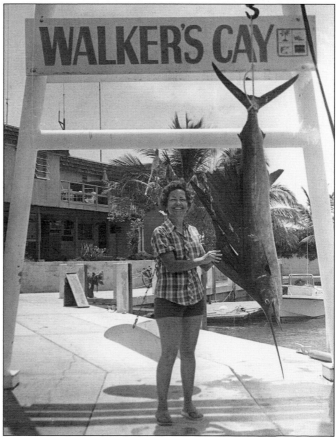

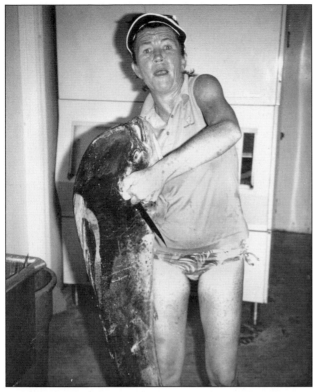

ALENE MOLLE. Alene is shown here with a bull dolphin that gave her the fight of her life. The large dolphin fought so hard it actually broke two of her ribs. Alene's facial expression shows the determination of a true angler. She and her husband, Vince "Smokey" Molle, owned and operated a restaurant called Smokey's on the Intracoastal Waterway in Boynton Beach. They still own the land where the Banana Boat restaurant is. (Courtesy Smokey and Alene Molle.)

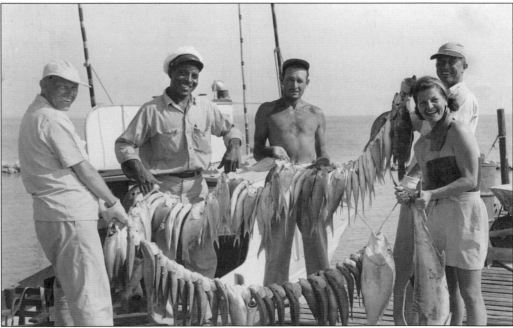

GREAT DAY FISHING. From left to right, Capt. C. C. "Bouncer" Anderson, an unidentified Walker's Cay guide, Capt. Jack Lance, and George and Phyllis Bass are all smiles as they display their catch of the day. A nice number of yellowtail snapper and a couple of amberjacks are held up for the camera. (Courtesy Bill Buckland's Fisherman's Center.)

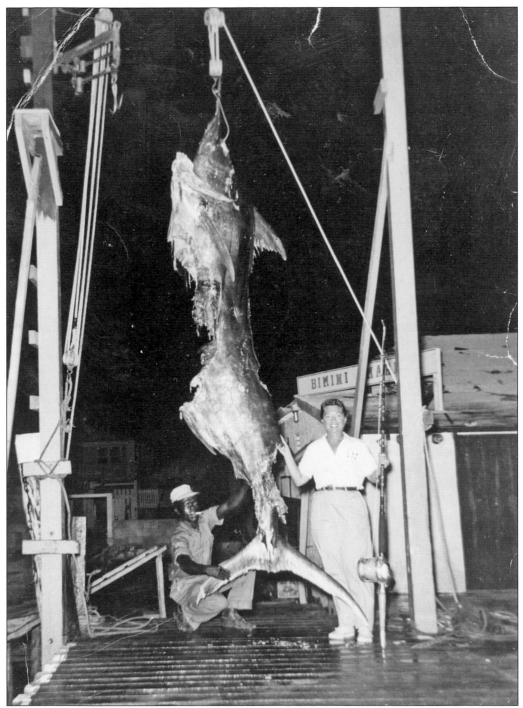

DOROTHEA LINCOLN DEANE. This is what was left of world-record holder Dorothea Lincoln Deane's blue marlin after sharks attacked it while she was boating the fish. The remains weighed 568 pounds and the girth was 68 inches. The measurement of the tail across was 46 inches. This catch really caused a sensation, as no one had ever seen a marlin this big. The photograph was taken in Bimini in 1958. (Courtesy Grady Stearns.)

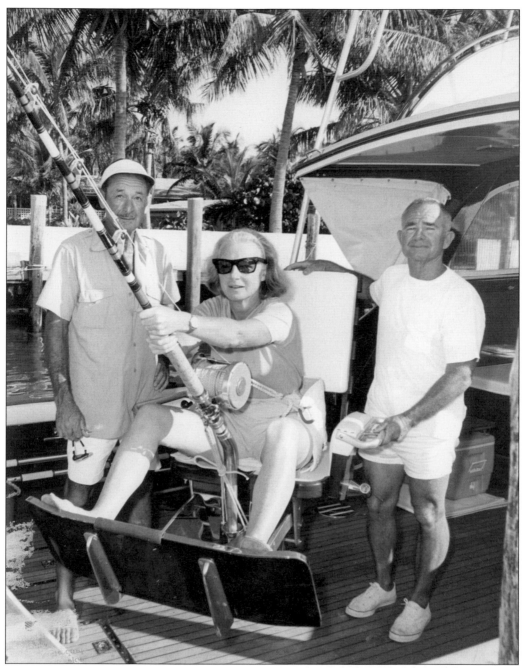

ANN C. KUNKEL. This early 1960s image of award-winning angler Ann C. Kunkel with Capt. Jack Lance (left) and Capt. Kenny Lyman (right) was taken during a fishing tournament in the Bahama Islands. Anne holds several International Game Fish Association (IGFA) world records. (Courtesy Lyman family.)

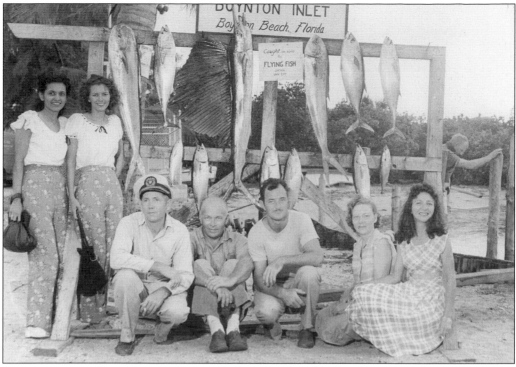

FAMILY AFFAIR. Sometimes boat captains brought their families along on fishing trips, or the wives would greet them at the dock. In Boynton, the women and families would often stand atop the inlet bridge and watch for the parade of boats returning after a day at sea. Gloria Galmiche "Gigi" Van Epp, wife of Capt. Corwin Van Epp, is the woman on the right in the checkered dress. (Courtesy Van Epp family.)

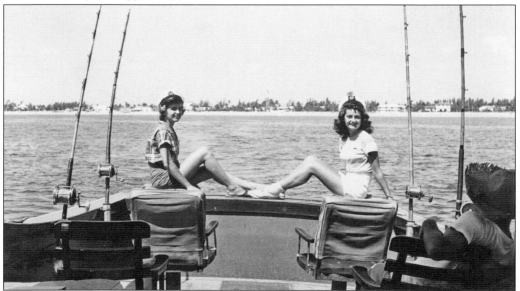

TROLLING ALONG. The fish might not be biting today, but Delores Snow (left) and Maxine Winn (right) seem to be enjoying their time on a sport fishing boat. The photograph is dated 1949. (Courtesy Delray Beach Historical Society.)

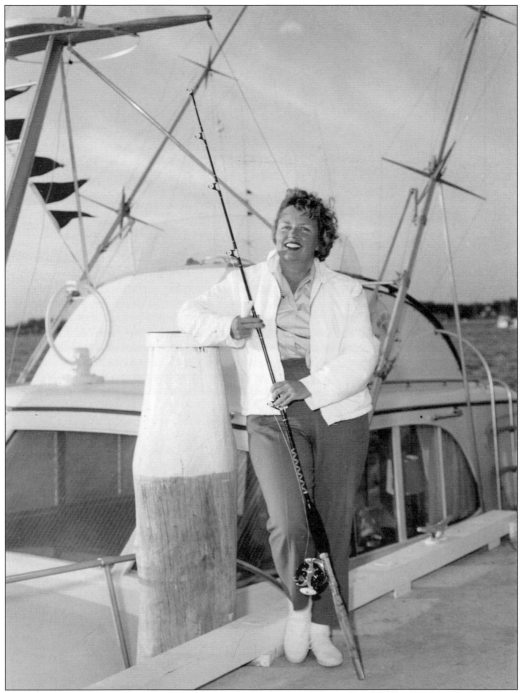

KAY RYBOVICH. In 1955, Kay Rybovich cofounded the International Woman's Fishing Association (IWFA). During the International Sailfish Tournament, Kay and friends Ginny Sherwood and Denny Crowninshield decided they loved fishing and wanted to fish more often than the occasional "ladies day." Ginny went to a lawyer and had the papers drawn up. Within one week, a group of 30 women anglers attended a meeting. The purpose was to promote fishing tournaments in many parts of the world. At one point, the IWFA boasted over 500 members. (Courtesy Kay Rybovich.)

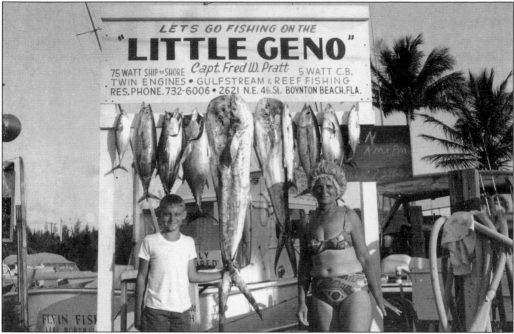

MAE PRATT. Both photographs on this page feature Mae Pratt of the *Little Geno*. The Little Geno Sport Fishing business was started by Capt. Fred Pratt and his wife, first mate Mae, out of the old Boynton Inlet in 1955. The boat was named after their son, Geno (above photograph, left), who was only three years old at the time. The Pratt family spent nearly every day together on the water, fishing and teaching others how to fish. In 1970, Captain Pratt upgraded his boat to a uniquely designed Chrisovich, which was a combination of Chris-Craft and Rybovich. The boat was one of only six of that design ever made. Today Geno continues in the family tradition; he and his wife, Karen, are the only known second-generation husband-and-wife team to run a charter boat. Their boat, *Geno III*, is docked at Lantana Sportsman Park. (Courtesy Pratt family.)

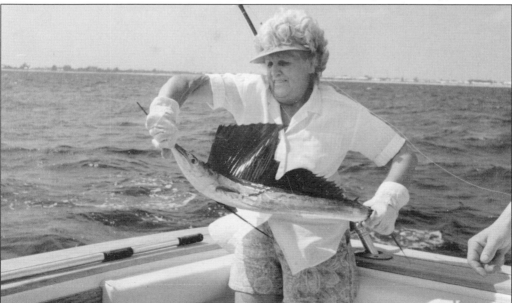

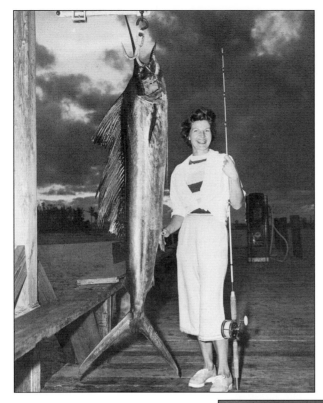

WORLD-RECORD SAILFISH.
Phyllis Bass, shown here with
her record sailfish, was the wife
of Birmingham, Michigan,
construction owner George A. Bass.
She was a member of the IWFA and
the WPBFC, and in her lifetime she
held 24 IGFA records. This mighty
fish was caught on the *Sambo*,
owned by her husband with Capt.
C. C. Anderson. Phyllis holds the
world record for sailfish using light
tackle. (Courtesy WPBFC.)

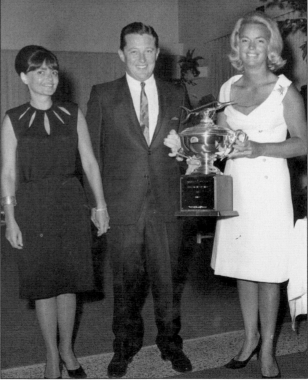

AWARD CEREMONY. IWFA and
WPBFC member Sandra Kaupe
poses with West Palm Beach
veterinarian Dr. Jack Liggett and
his wife, Grace. The photograph
was taken at the Sailfish Club of
Florida in Palm Beach. (Courtesy
Jack Liggett.)

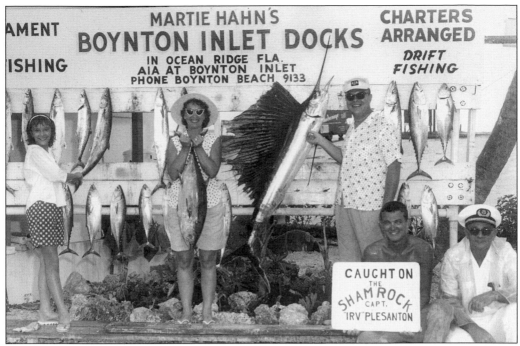

MOTHER AND DAUGHTER. A mother and daughter duo appears delighted with their bounty aboard the charter boat *Shamrock* with Capt. Irv Pleasanton. The *Shamrock* docked at Martie Hahn's Boynton Inlet Docks in Ocean Ridge. (Courtesy Jimmy Duncan.)

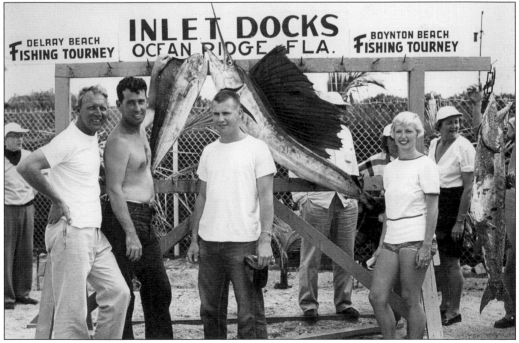

LADY LUCK. A young lady wearing short shorts in this 1960s-era photograph poses with a dolphin, sailfish, and barracuda. Perhaps the lady brought these tournament anglers luck. Capt. Homer Adams is on the far left. (Courtesy Shirley Adams.)

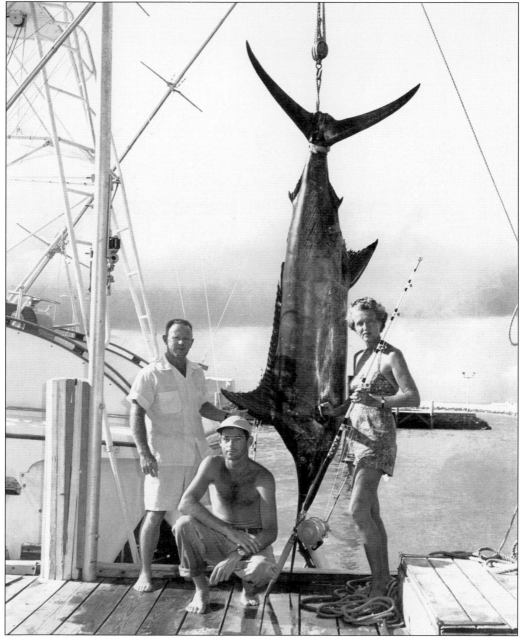

CYNTHIA BOOMHOWER. Boomhower, a longtime WPBFC and IWFA member and IGFA world-record holder, is shown here with her first blue marlin. The 324-pound fish was caught aboard her boat, the 37-foot Rybovich CB, in June 1957. Also pictured are Capt. Red McBride (left) and mate Frank Cote. (Courtesy WPBFC.)

Four

PIER, BEACH, AND JETTY FISHING

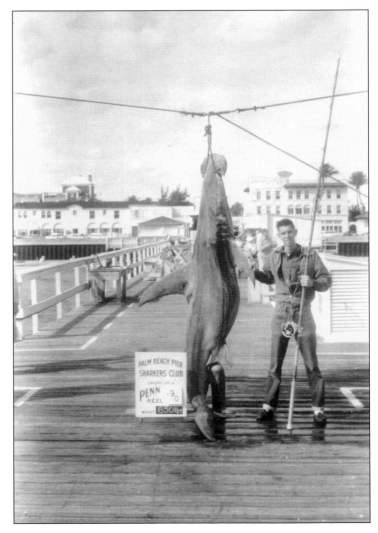

SHARK FISHING. Sixteen-year-old Jim Barry is on the Palm Beach Pier with his 850-pound hammerhead shark, for which he won a Penn Reel Trophy. The Palm Beach Pier, built in 1920 by Gus Jordahn, was originally called Rainbow Pier and was in existence from 1923 to 1966 at the end of Worth Avenue. The pier master was George Debay, who ran a tackle shop and taught many kids to fish. (Courtesy Jim Barry.)

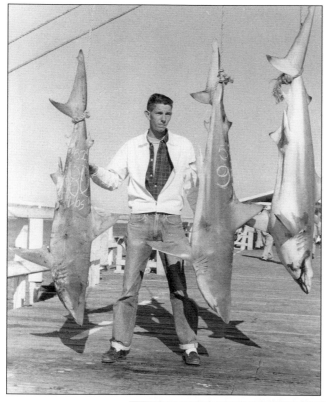

JIM BARRY. Jim Barry, shown here, was a member of the Palm Beach Pier Sharkers Club and landed about 300 big sharks off the Palm Beach and Juno Piers during his years as a sharker. He grew up in Palm Beach County, attended the University of Miami, earned a degree in marine biology, and became director the Palm Beach County Department of Environmental Resources Management. Barry retired from ERM in 2006. Barry dedicated his life to conservation efforts and is the person most responsible for all the good things that have happened to the restoration of the Lake Worth Lagoon. (Courtesy Jim Barry.)

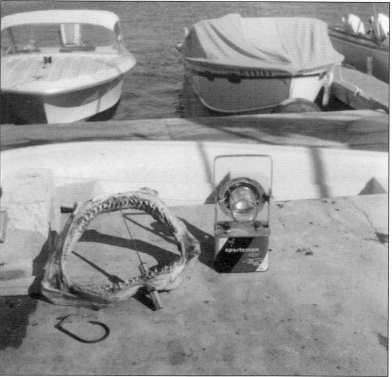

JAWS. This is one of the shark jaws that Jim Barry collected and sold. In 1963, he sold jaws for $20 to $25 a set, which paid more money than a paper route. Additionally, since sharks have six or seven rows of teeth and four to seven of the rows are hollow, he sold three rows of the 50 solid teeth for $7.50. (Courtesy Jim Barry.)

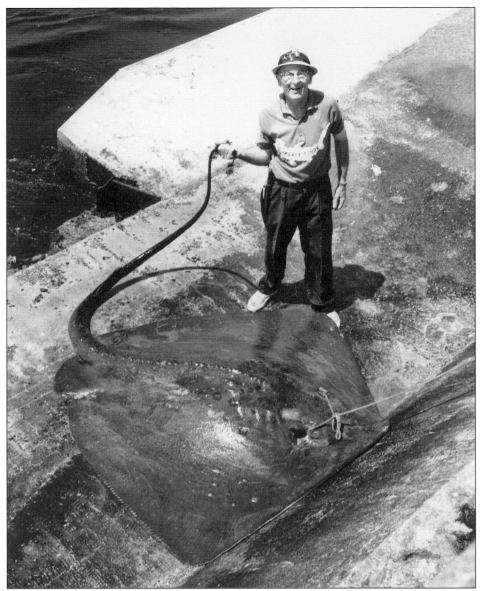

SHARK MAN OF LAKE WORTH. Herb Goodman, shown here, spent 35 years fishing for sharks. He landed his first one in 1948 by mistake. While he was surf fishing for pompano, a small fish, a shark took a bite of the fish he was reeling in. Eventually he began fishing with a stout surf rod and 130-pound test line. He once caught a 475-pound hammerhead, pregnant with 29 pups. Herb often had an audience, and with strength, patience, innovative techniques and imaginative angles, he reeled in 177 sharks, all longer than six feet, during his career. Today sharks around the world are in trouble from overfishing, and catch-and-release is now encouraged. Herb Goodman, whose license plate read, "Sharky-1," was quite a showman and was featured in publications as far away as Sydney, Australia. He built a little motorized boat he called the Ray-O-Vac Craft to transport his bait out to deep water. The Ray-O-Vac people supplied the batteries and tackle distributors donated some of his gear. In this photograph, Goodman has an unusual catch—not a shark this time, but a large sting ray. (Courtesy Museum of the City of Lake Worth.)

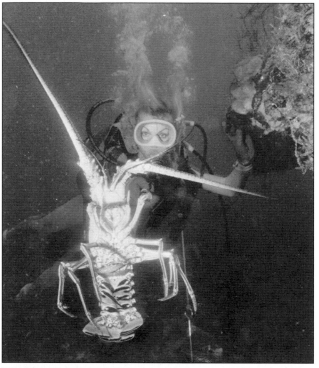

LOBSTER DIVING. Linda Reeves, a photojournalist and local diver, has been catching, eating, and researching the Florida lobster for many years. The spiny lobster has been commercially fished with traps for about 100 years. The 1950s brought the production of scuba equipment, enabling hunters to go to the depths with nets, spears, and snares, which presented overfishing and environmental issues. Since the 1980s, a two-day sport diver season has put regulations on measuring, bag limits, and fishing tools. (Courtesy Linda Reeves.)

BUGGED OUT. This is another great underwater shot showing brothers John (right) and Jim Jolley diving for lobster off the Gulf Stream Clubhouse in 1963. (Courtesy John Jolley.)

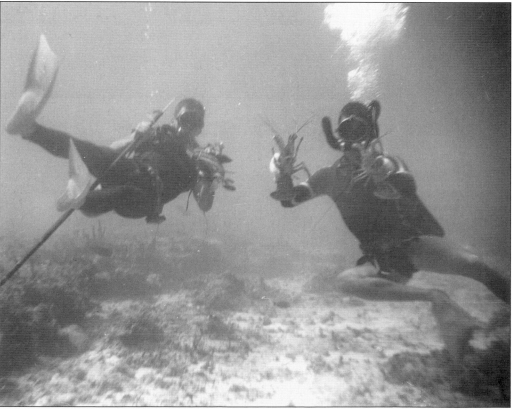

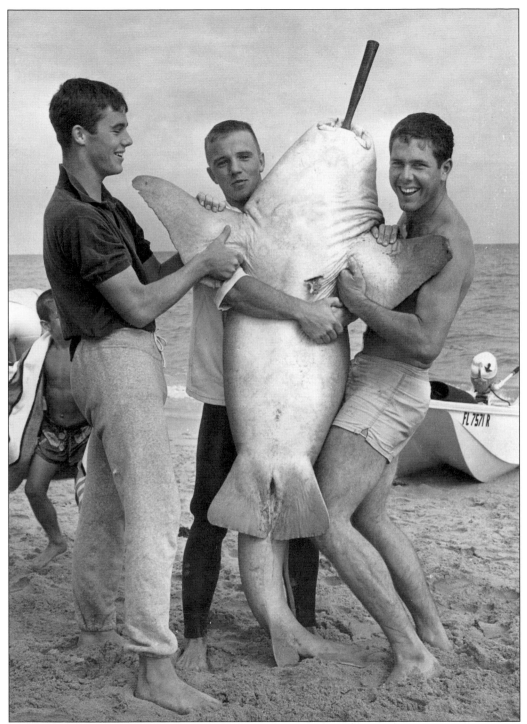

GREAT CATCH. Pictured from left to right, John Jolley, Mike Hill, and Jim Dutcher hold a nurse shark speared off Delray Beach. James Dutcher now is a famous cinematographer, and his works include *The Water Cycle*, *On Beaver Pond*, and the Discovery Channel documentary *Living with Wolves*. (Courtesy John Jolley.)

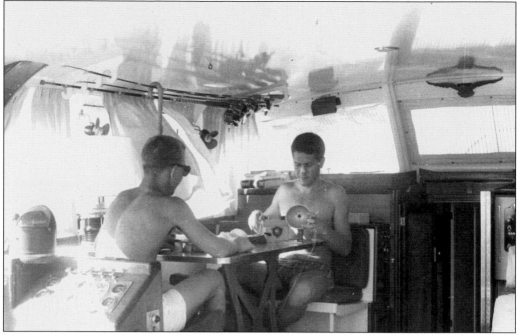

UNDERWATER PHOTOGRAPHY. Note the intense looks on the faces of Jim Dutcher (right) and Mike Hill of Delray Beach as they load their underwater cameras in 1961. The photograph was taken in Bimini, Bahamas. This image shows the early development of Jim Dutcher's photographic career. He is now one of the most famous wildlife photographers in the world. (Courtesy John Jolley.)

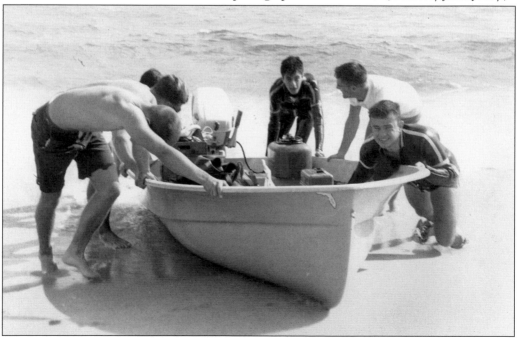

EXPLORING THE COAST. In the early 1960s, the reefs off Palm Beach County were teeming with marine life, and many of the local teens would take small boats offshore and dive. This photograph shows a group of young men coming ashore after diving all day. (Courtesy John Jolley.)

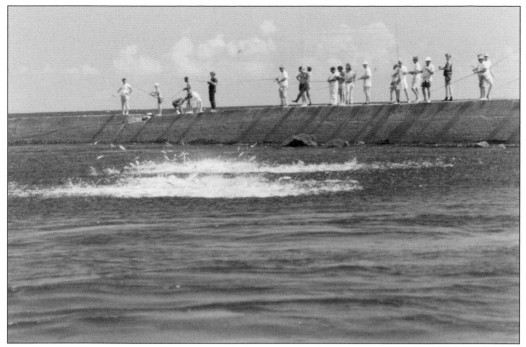

JETTY CONCH TRADITION. The Jetty Conchs started in the 1940s as a group of fishing friends who followed the migrating mullet in early September each year. The south jetty of the Palm Beach Inlet was the official place for these folks, who would appear at the inlet dock once a year just as the northeast winds began to blow. The Jetty Conchs were from all walks of life—a carpet layer, a district attorney, a house painter, and so on. They used special rods strong enough to cast a mullet and hook a snook. The Jetty Conchs met annually from about 1955 to 1980. (Courtesy Jim Branch.)

STRANGE CATCH. Jim Branch snared this combination snook. While he was pursuing mullet, the open-mouthed snook ran into a traffic jam and another snook, going the wrong way through a thoroughfare of schooling mullet, became lodged in its mouth. Together the fish weighed 18 pounds. Newspapers picked up the story and claimed he made angling history with a two-in-one snook. The photograph was taken in front of George DeBay's Sport Shop on the Palm Beach Pier. (Courtesy Jim Branch.)

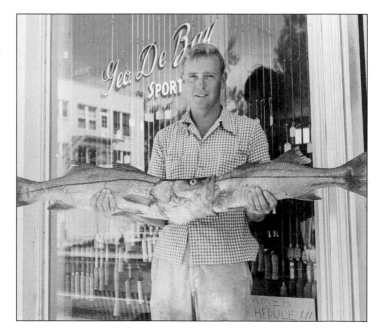

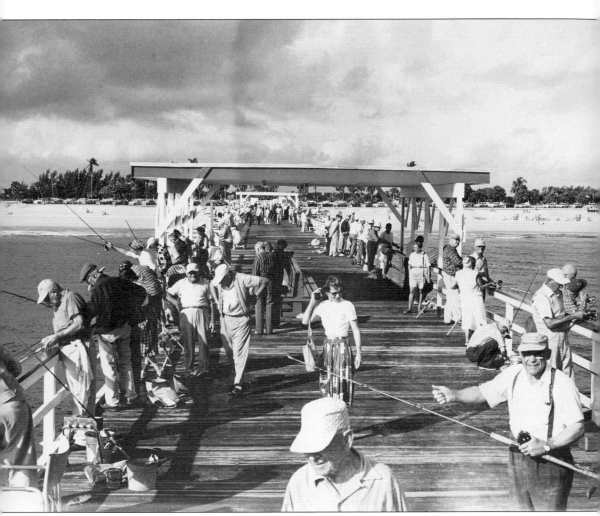

LAKE WORTH PIER. Dozens of anglers are shown fishing from the Lake Worth Pier. Ground was broken for the Lake Worth casino, bathhouse, and pier on August 18, 1921, and it was dedicated in June 1922. In 1954, the 300-foot pier, one of the longest municipal piers on Florida's Atlantic Coast, opened to the public. (Courtesy Museum of the City of Lake Worth.)

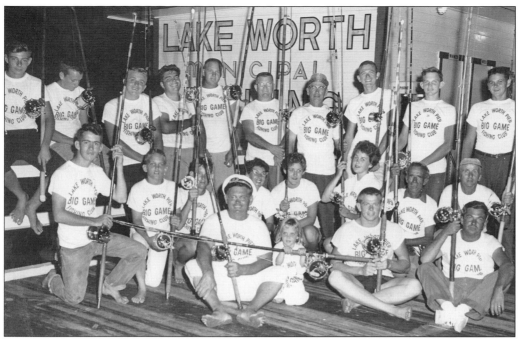

FISHING CLUB. Members of the Lake Worth Pier Big Game Fishing Club pose with their rods on the William O. Lockhart Municipal Pier in the 1960s. (Courtesy Capt. Jimmy Duncan.)

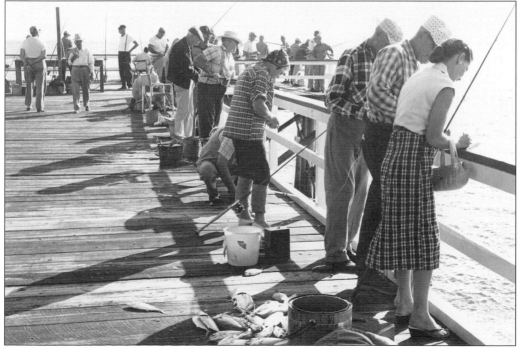

WILLIAM O. LOCKHART MUNICIPAL PIER. The popular William O. Lockhart Lake Worth Municipal Pier was filled with anglers on most days until the hurricanes of 2004 ripped it apart. Murphy's Construction began the rebuilding process in 2007. (Courtesy Museum of the City of Lake Worth.)

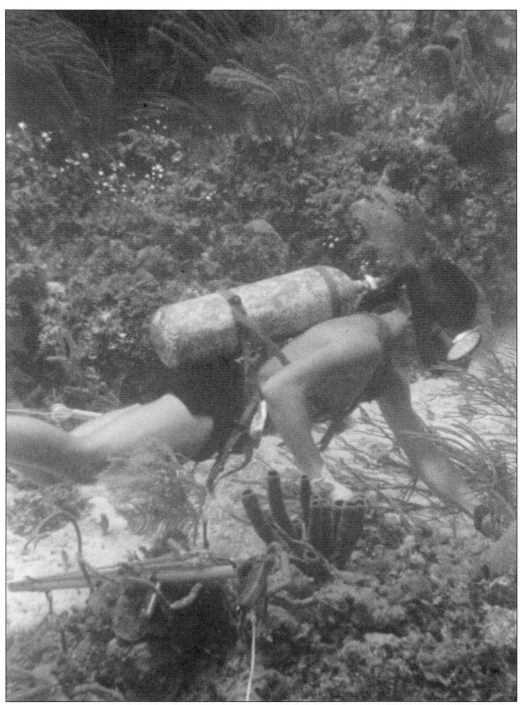

UNDERWATER EXPLORATION. Exploring the natural beauty of the area while diving the backside reefs in 75 feet of water off Manalapan is Delray Beach teenager John Jolley. He is searching for grouper using a homemade spear gun in this 1962 photograph. (Courtesy John Jolley.)

Five

FISHING FESTIVITIES

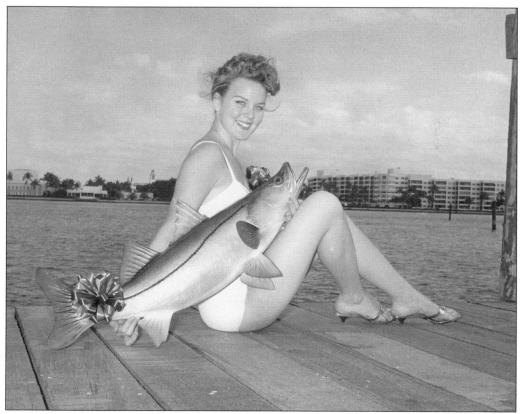

PRIZED CATCH. Fishing activities in Palm Beach County encompass much more than the actual time on the water. Celebrations, parades, fish fries, tournaments, and beauty pageants are some traditions involving families and community members in the sport of fishing. The young lady shown here with the beribboned snook is a model helping to draw attention to big game fishing. (Courtesy WPBFC.)

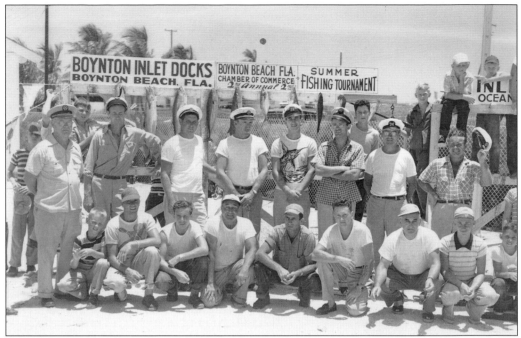

CAPTAINS AND KIDS. A group of captains, mates, and children gather on opening day of the second annual Boynton Beach Chamber of Commerce Summer Fishing Tournament. Capt. Herb Schulz is the man standing third from the left, with Capt. Jack Williams on his right, and Capt. Kenny Lyman is the man standing on the right waving his cap. (Courtesy Lyman family.)

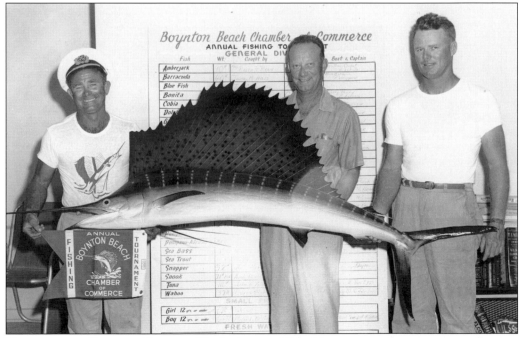

TOURNAMENT DIVISION ROSTER. Displaying a sailfish skin mount and a tournament flag are, from left to right, Capt. Kenny Lyman, angler Doc Rhoden, and Capt. Red Waggener. Behind them is a chart used to record winning data. (Courtesy Lyman family.)

CORNELL WILDE. Dashing actor
Cornell Wilde wears a pair of gloves
as he holds up his sailfish catch in
this promotional photograph. Wilde,
an Academy Award nominee for his
1945 role in *A Song to Remember*,
is assisted by a model wearing the
proverbial teeny-weenie polka-dot
bikini. (Courtesy WPBFC.)

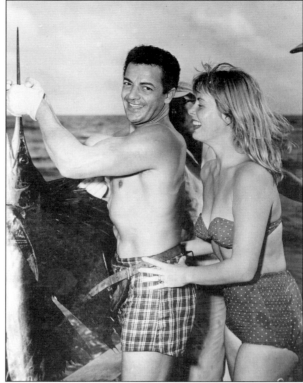

SAILFISH GRUDGE MATCH. This
1950s-era photograph shows
professional golfer Sam Snead
(left) and major league baseball
legend Ted Williams (right) in a
promotional photograph for the
sailfish grudge match. This famous
event, held by the WPBFC, was
designed to attract media attention
and tourists to Palm Beach County
and promote the Silver Sailfish
Derby. New Jersey *Star Ledger* writer
Nelson Benedict is the man in the
center. (Courtesy WPBFC.)

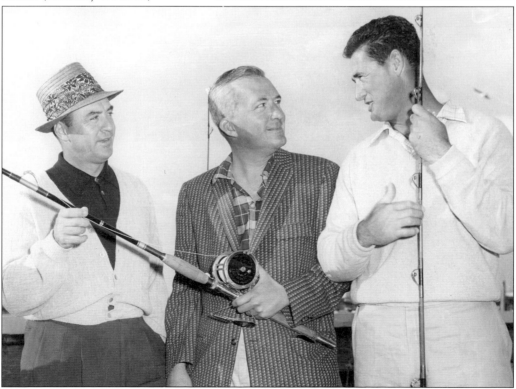

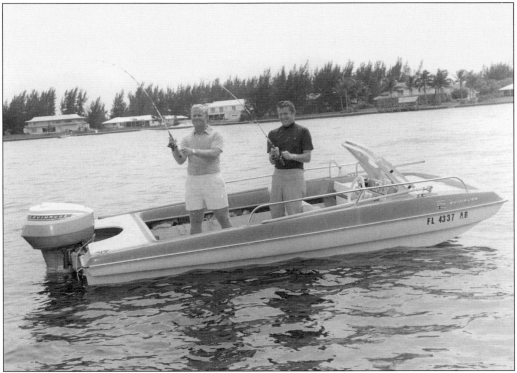

JACK NICKLAUS. Many celebrities enjoy fishing in beautiful Palm Beach County. Bob Davidoff took this 1960s photograph of golf legend Jack Nicklaus (left) and West Palm Beach veterinarian Dr. Jack Liggett fishing in the Lake Worth Lagoon. Dr. Liggett taught Jack big game fishing, and the pair have fished in many parts of the world. There are over 200 different species of fish in the inland waterway. (Courtesy Davidoff Studios.)

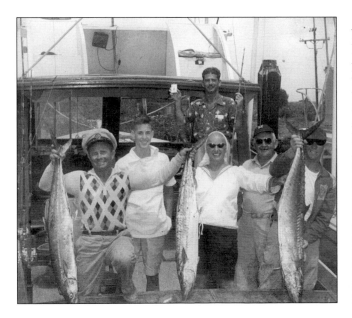

FAYE EMERSON. Actress Faye Emerson smiles in this 1950s photograph. The lovely Emerson was a television personality as well as a film and stage actress. She married Elliot Roosevelt, son of Pres. Franklin Delano Roosevelt, in 1944. In 1951, she married Lyle C. "Skitch" Henderson. Capt. Jack Smith of the television show *Fin and Fun* is in the background. He likely featured Emerson on his program. Pictured from left to right in front are Capt. Kenny Lyman, Faye Emerson's son, Faye Emerson, Les Curfman, and mate Jimmy Lunsford. (Courtesy Lyman family.)

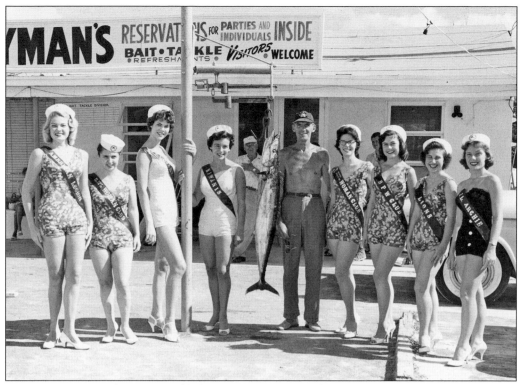

BEAUTY QUEENS. These nautical ladies posing in front of the entrance to Lyman's Sport Fishing Docks are representing various community businesses and civic groups. The pageant was a huge tradition that continued well into the 1970s. Local newspapers of the era are filled with tidbits about tournaments and festivities both before and after the exciting events. (Courtesy Lyman family.)

PAGEANTRY PARODY. Not to be outdone by the ladies, local men bravely pose on Lyman's docks in a mock beauty contest. The man second from the right is Capt. Wendall Hall. The "contestants" sport names like Miss-Hap, Miss America, Miss-Take, and Miss-Doubt. The girl in the center is Nancy DiMorrow. (Courtesy Janet Hall.)

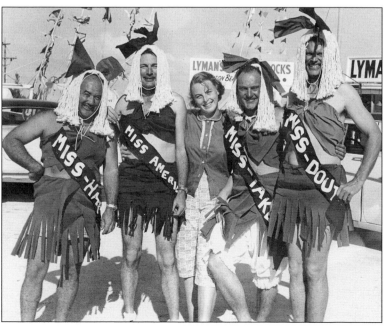

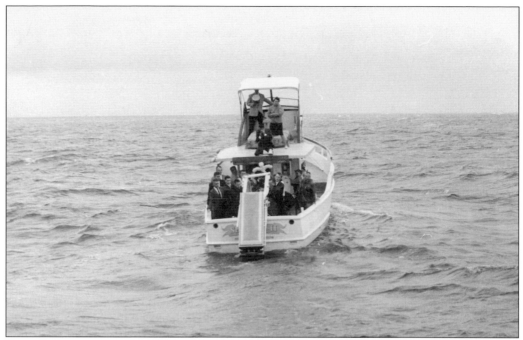

SOMBER CELEBRATION. Both photographs on this page are from a 1950s burial at sea. One of the mates on the *Sea-Mist*, Jim Ross, passed away, and friends and family honor his wishes. Legally a captain can bury remains at sea provided that environmental regulations are satisfied. In the United States, ashes have to be scattered at least 3 miles offshore, and the location must be at least 600 feet deep. (Courtesy Janet Hall.)

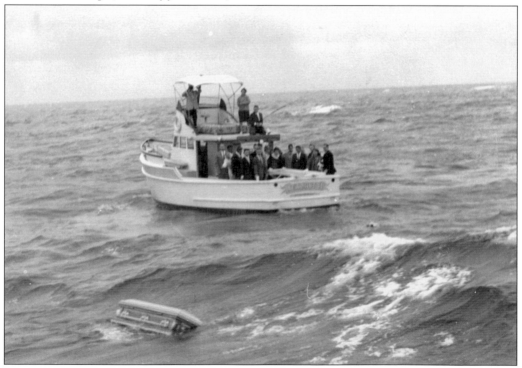

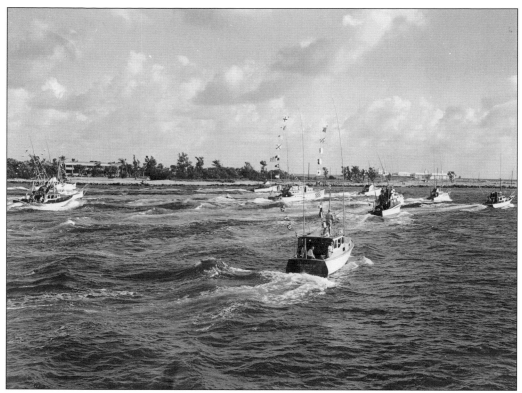

BIMINI START. One of the most festive traditions in many big fishing tournaments is a Bimini Start. Here boats participating in the famed Silver Sailfish Derby are leaving the inland waterway through the Palm Beach Inlet and racing out to sea. Some of the boats display colorful flags. (Courtesy WPBFC.)

JAMES MELTON. Another fishing festivity in Boynton Beach was when James Melton brought some of his antique cars down to the sport fishing docks. Crowds of people gathered at the popular dock to see the automobiles and the pretty girls. Miss Florida is the lovely lady beside famed tenor James Melton. (Courtesy Lyman family.)

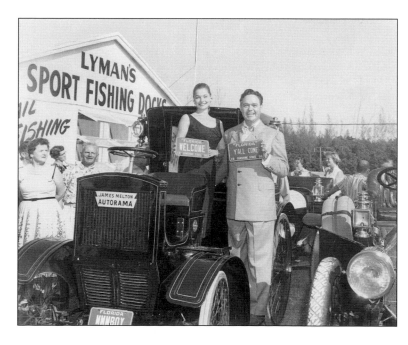

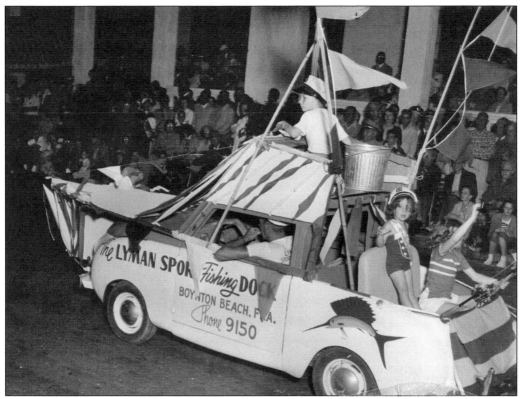

PARADE. A small truck has been transformed into a boat, complete with outriggers, for a parade. Walter "Skipper" Lyman is on the flying bridge. A garbage can next to him is full of paper airplanes advertising the Lyman Sport Fishing Docks. Cindy Lyman Jamison is the girl wearing the captain's hat, and Martha "Marti" Lunsford McPherson is beside Cindy waving to the crowd. Don Lyman is driving the car. (Courtesy Lyman family.)

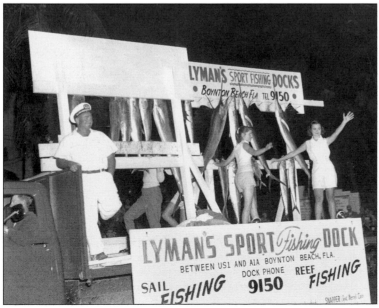

PARADE OF FISH. Capt. Kenny Lyman is shown aboard a parade float advertising his sport fishing dock. The girls dancing and waving to spectators are Marti Lunsford McPherson (center) and Joan Arnold (right). Captain Lyman gave his parade entry added authenticity by adding a rack of fish to the float. (Courtesy Lyman family.)

FISH FRY.
Celebrations and fund-raisers often included a fish fry. Some captains would keep extra kingfish on ice and then donate the fish for a community event. This one on Lyman's Sport Fishing Docks included music and dancing. (Courtesy Lyman family.)

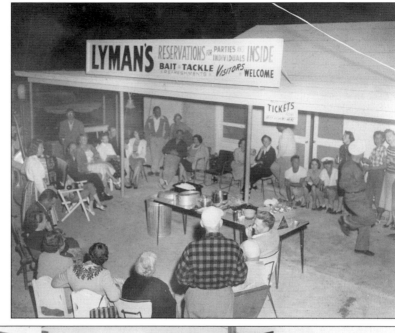

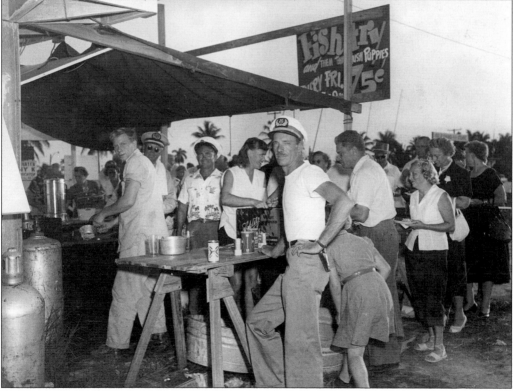

FISH AND HUSH PUPPIES. A long line of hungry people look forward to fresh fish and deep-fried hush puppies. This undated photograph has a sign indicating a fish fry held every Friday night. The Kiwanis and other community and civic groups often held such events. In the 1950s, an adult ticket was 75¢ for all the fish and hush puppies one could eat. (Courtesy Lyman family.)

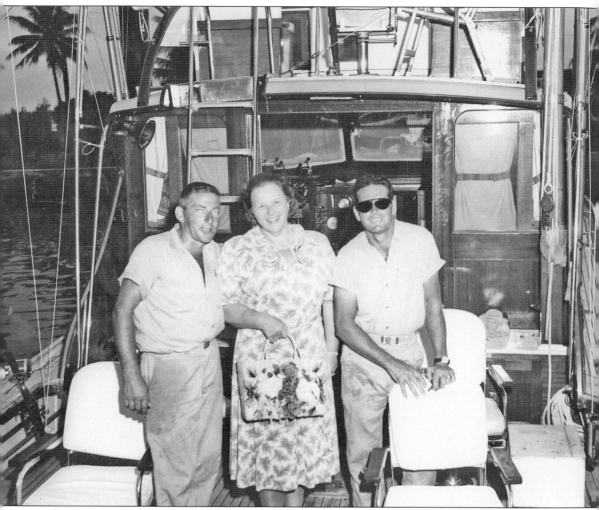

KATE SMITH. Enjoying some time in Palm Beach County is singer Kate Smith, best known for her rendition of Irving Berlin's "God Bless America." She was one of America's most beloved entertainers, with a radio, television, and recording career that spanned five decades. Smith was known for her big voice and big figure. Proceeds from her performances of "God Bless America" were donated to the Boy Scouts and Girl Scouts. She and her son must have enjoyed big game fishing with Capt. Bob Raven Ridgeway (right) and mate Pete Volcanas (left) on the *Sally Shall III*. (Courtesy Janet Hall.)

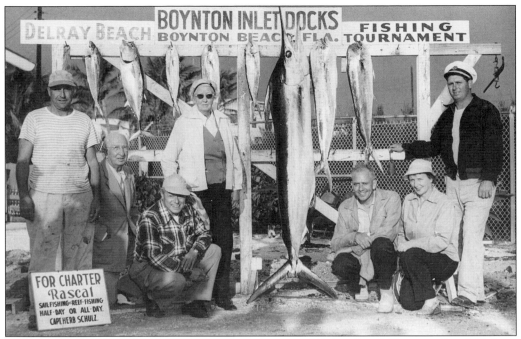

TOURNAMENT TIME. This photograph is from the annual Delray Beach/Boynton Beach Fishing Tournament. The tourney was just one of the many fishing competitions held in Palm Beach County. Capt. Herb Schulz is on the right in the above photograph and on the left in the image below. The catch behind him includes a blue marlin and numerous dolphin. (Courtesy Shirley Adams.)

FISHING JAMBOREE. From 1957 to 1965, hundreds of Palm Beach County children participated in the Bev Smith Ford Kruise Kids program. Each year a big Kruise Kids Jamboree was held at Bill's Sailfish Marina, and local charter boats would join forces to give more kids a special day. Several thousand youngsters have special memories of their day saltwater fishing and the traditional picnic fare of hot dogs, chips, and bottles of cold soda afterwards. (Courtesy Vern Pickup Crawford.)

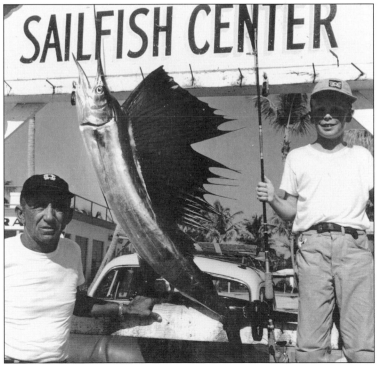

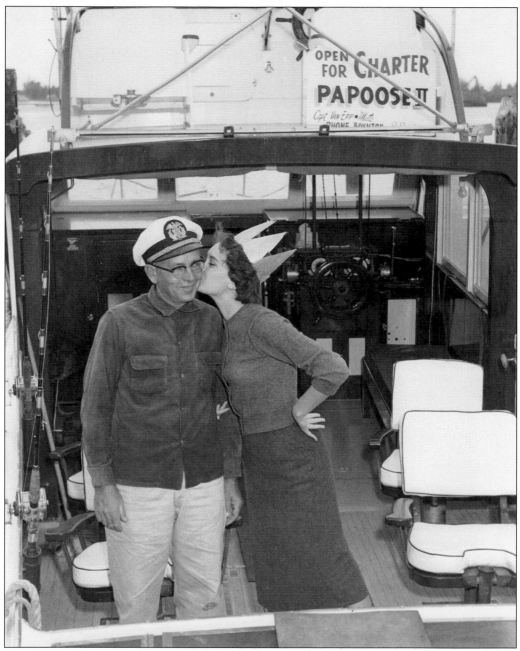

KISS FROM A QUEEN. Capt. Corwin Van Epp receives a kiss from one of the contestants in the annual Miss Boynton Beach Fishing Tournament Pageant. The contest was sponsored by the Boynton Beach Chamber of Commerce. The classic photograph was taken aboard Capt. Van Epps charter boat *Papoose II*. (Courtesy Donald Van Epp.)

Six

BUSINESSES
SUPPORTING FISHING

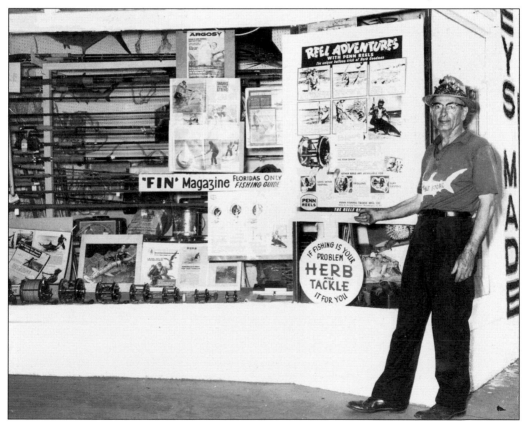

HERB'S TACKLE SHOP. One of the many little tackle shops in Palm Beach County and perhaps one of the best known was Herb's Key Shop on Lake Avenue in Lake Worth. Operated by Louis "Herb" Goodman, the store sold Penn reels, *Fin* Magazine, and shark teeth and jaws. His slogan was, "If fishing is your problem, Herb will tackle it for you." Co-fixtures on Lake Avenue for over 40 years, Herb, known as "Shark Man of Lake Worth," and Herb's Key Shop are fondly remembered by generations of fishermen. (Courtesy Museum of the City of Lake Worth.)

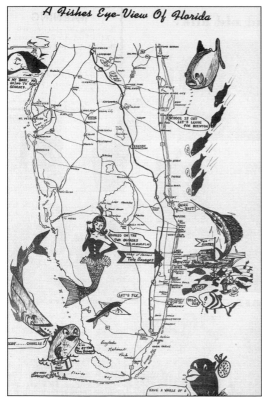

A Fishes Eye-View Of Florida

FISH'S VIEW. In the 1950s, 1960s, and 1970s, local newspapers ran detailed weekly accounts about fishing. A cartoonist for the *Boynton Beach Star*, Mike Giersher, drew many cartoons about fishing. This early 1960s drawing illustrates the record number of fish in Palm Beach County waters. (Courtesy Boynton Beach City Library Archive.)

CHAMBER OF COMMERCE AD. This 1960s Boynton Beach Chamber of Commerce advertisement entices visitors and newcomers to "Relax and Enjoy Living." The brochure puts emphasis on the great location and on fishing. While the smiling swimsuit model Pat Gardner, Miss Boynton Beach 1965, standing at the edge of the Intracoastal Waterway, may reel in the reader, the words tout Boynton Beach to be the "Gateway to Sailfish Alley, World Famous Gulf Stream Fishing in Fabulous Palm Beach County." (Courtesy Boynton Beach City Library Archives.)

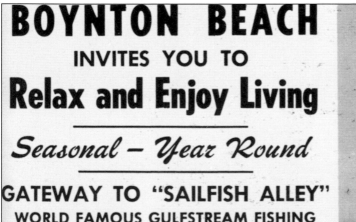

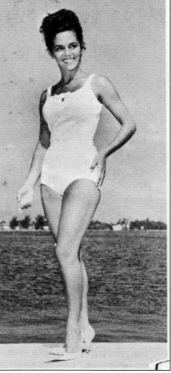

TELEVISION PERSONALITY.
Vern Crawford came to
West Palm Beach in 1939,
working briefly at WJNO
radio until he volunteered
for the army in 1941.
Crawford was the first voice
heard on local television
in 1954, when Phipps
Broadcasting opened WJNO-
TV Channel 5. WJNO
became WPTV in 1956.
Crawford was chief director
for live programming and
the premier television/radio
fishing reporter from 1954
to 1958. (Courtesy Vern
Pickup Crawford.)

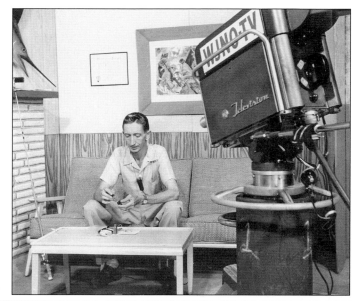

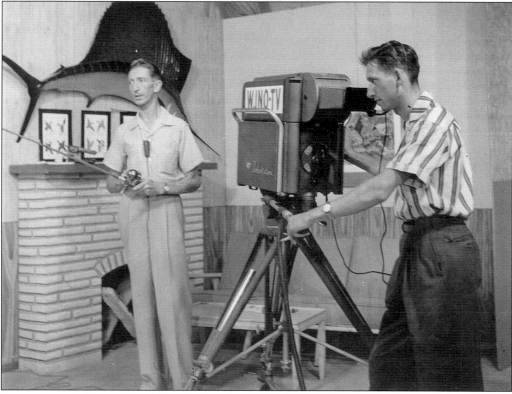

FISHING WITH VERN. Vern Crawford is shown on the set of WPTV in 1957. His first fishing
show was *Reel, Keel and Rifle*, then going on to *Fishing with Vern*, before changing it to simply
the *Fishing Report* during his last years. Crawford hosted a series of fishing programs until April
1980, when he had to leave for health reasons. He would visit just about every charter and drift
boat captain from Riviera to Boynton daily or weekly, as well as the Juno, Palm Beach, and Lake
Worth piers. (Courtesy Vern Pickup Crawford.)

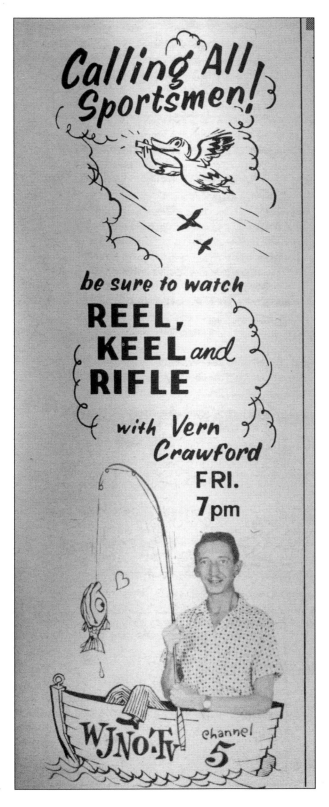

REEL, KEEL AND RIFLE SHOW.
This was a 1956 advertisement for the popular *Reel, Keel and Rifle* show with Vern Crawford. The half-hour program aired on WJNO-TV Channel 5 Friday evenings at 7:00 p.m. The ad portrays Vern Crawford in a small cartoon-like boat with a fishing rod. It begins with the message, "Calling All Sportsmen!" (Courtesy Vern Pickup Crawford.)

KRUISE KIDS TELEVISION PROGRAM. Vern Crawford's wife, Lee, did the first weather program on WPTV called *Lee Side of the Weather.* Together the Crawfords hosted the original *Kruise Kids* Thursday evening television show, sponsored by Bev Smith Ford. This 1956 photograph is of a game segment on the show. Lee is holding up a fish, and Vern is guiding the game contestant onto center stage. (Courtesy Vern Pickup Crawford.)

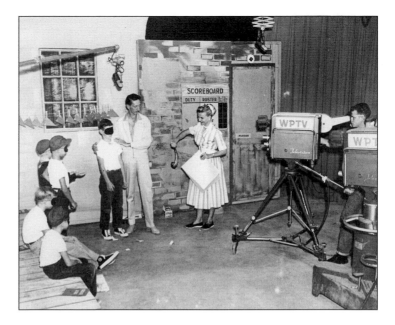

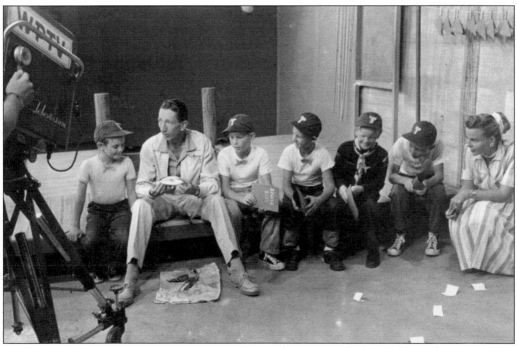

THURSDAY NIGHT TELEVISION SHOW. Vern and Lee Crawford are shown here with five youngsters during the weekly *Kruise Kids* show. The boys are wearing name tags in the shape of fish, and Vern Crawford is holding up a small fish. One of the many fishing concepts the show taught was catch-and-release. Vern "Sandy" Pickup Crawford is the boy in the Cub Scout uniform. Young Sandy sometimes filled in on the show when there was an empty spot. (Courtesy Vern Pickup Crawford.)

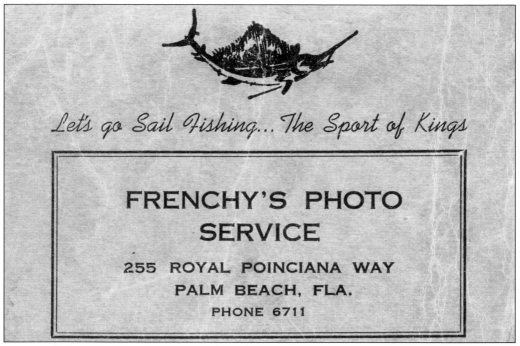

Let's go Sail Fishing... The Sport of Kings

FRENCHY'S PHOTO SERVICE

255 ROYAL POINCIANA WAY
PALM BEACH, FLA.
PHONE 6711

FRENCHY'S PHOTO SERVICE. Many anglers who visited Palm Beach County wanted souvenirs of their prized catch. Photographs documenting the fishing experience were taken by dockworkers and local photographers. Some local businesses even created small scrapbooks and albums of fishing adventures. Frenchy's Photo Service in Palm Beach had a special album for anglers. The 12-page booklet's cover included a drawing of a sailfish and the inscription, "Let's go Sail Fishing . . . The Sport of Kings." (Courtesy Shirley Adams.)

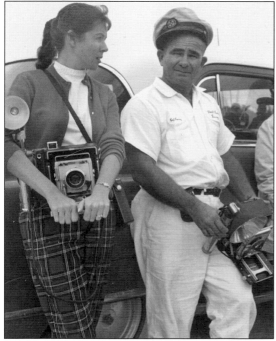

FROZEN IN TIME. Fishing tournaments, special events, and daily fishing excursions were well documented throughout the 1950s, 1960s, and 1970s. Dozens of local photographers frequented the docks and marinas and made money selling photographs to the visitors. The dockmaster often received a complimentary copy of the photographs. Here Capt. Kenny Lyman of Boynton Beach and a female photographer stand side by side, each of them ready to capture a historic moment frozen in time. (Courtesy Lyman family.)

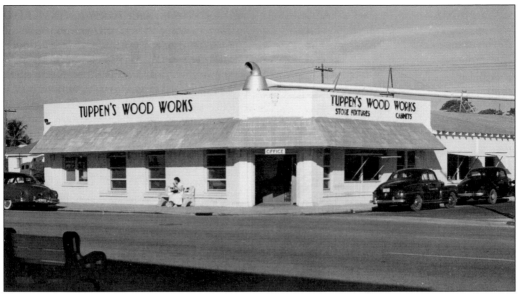

TUPPEN'S WOOD WORKS. Shown here is the original Tuppen's store at 1002 North Dixie Highway in Lake Worth. Sherman and Mildred Tuppen emigrated from Finland and started the business, originally called Tuppen's Wood Works. They created and sold wood molding and cabinets in the late 1940s. The business expanded to build wood boats. In 1956, the shop was renamed Tuppen's Sporting Goods. (Courtesy Buddy Tuppen.)

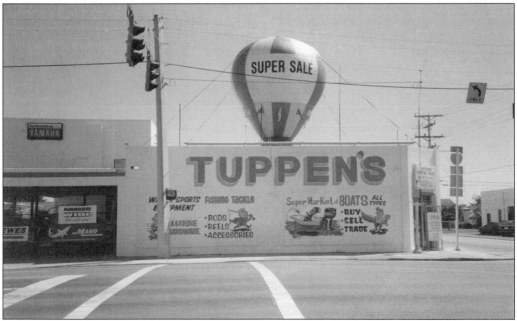

TUPPEN'S SPORTING GOODS. Tuppen's Sporting Goods store, shown here in the 1960s, is somewhat of an institution in Palm Beach County as well as a local landmark. Three generations of Tuppens worked here. The store sold tackle and Penn rods and reels. Boats of wood as well as aluminum were made at the shop. Sons Ron and Buddy attended Lake Worth High School. After attending the University of Florida, Buddy went to mechanics school to learn to work on Evinrude outboard motors. (Courtesy Buddy Tuppen.)

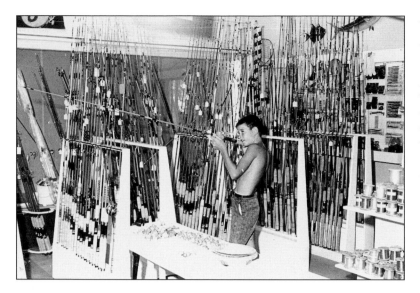

RODS AND REELS. A young fisherman examines one of the many rods on display at the Tuppen's Sporting Goods store. One of the most popular rods was a Mitchell 300 spin rod. In 1968, a combination rod and reel was priced at $16.95. (Courtesy Buddy Tuppen.)

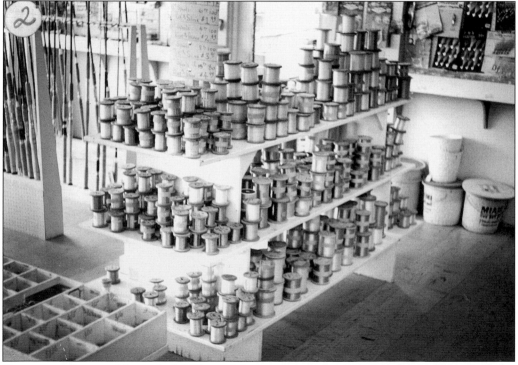

OODLES OF SPOOLS. Not only did Tuppen's have a great selection of quality reels, in 1960 the store also had many kinds of fishing line in stock, as seen here on plywood spools. The employees would give individual attention and advice to each customer and would spool the reels for them. Bait buckets and jig lures are displayed along the back wall. (Courtesy Buddy Tuppen.)

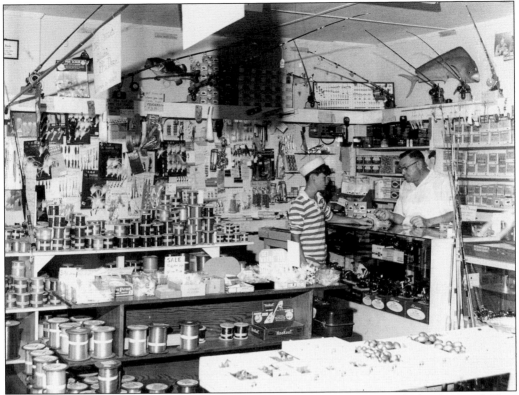

CUSTOMER SERVICE. Businesses back in the day before chain stores were mostly family owned. Here a longtime employee of Tuppen's Sporting Goods serves a young customer. Notice all the old store stock hanging from the walls and the reels displayed in the glass case. (Courtesy Buddy Tuppen.)

BOAT SERVICE AND SALES. Tuppen's also sold boats and engines. Before the Tuppen family bought the building, it was an old Ford garage. This 1960s image shows the interior of the engine shop and an unidentified employee working on an engine. In 1968, a nice boat with motor sold for $1,695. After 47 years in business, the store was sold but still operates at Tuppen's Marine and is an authorized Yahama service center. (Courtesy Buddy Tuppen.)

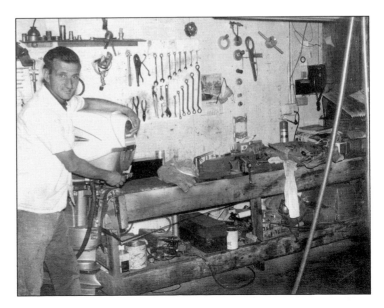

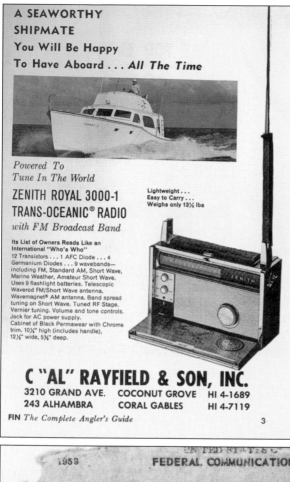

A SEAWORTHY
SHIPMATE
You Will Be Happy
To Have Aboard . . . All The Time

Powered To
Tune In The World

ZENITH ROYAL 3000-1
TRANS-OCEANIC® RADIO
with FM Broadcast Band

Lightweight . . .
Easy to Carry . . .
Weighs only 13¼ lbs

Its List of Owners Reads Like an
International "Who's Who"
12 Transistors . . . 1 AFC Diode . . . 4
Germanium Diodes . . . 9 wavebands—
including FM, Standard AM, Short Wave,
Marine Weather, Amateur Short Wave.
Uses 9 flashlight batteries. Telescopic
Wavered FM/Short Wave antenna.
Wavemagnet® AM antenna. Band spread
tuning on Short Wave. Tuned RF Stage.
Vernier tuning. Volume and tone controls.
Jack for AC power supply.
Cabinet of Black Permawear with Chrome
trim. 10¼" high (includes handle),
12½" wide, 5¾" deep.

C "AL" RAYFIELD & SON, INC.
3210 GRAND AVE.   COCONUT GROVE   HI 4-1689
243 ALHAMBRA   CORAL GABLES   HI 4-7119

FIN *The Complete Angler's Guide*   3

TRANS-OCEANIC RADIO. This 1964 advertisement was for a popular portable shortwave radio, the Zenith Royal 3001-1 Trans-oceanic Radio. Zenith Radio produced many different types of radios, but in late 1957 the first transistorized radio was introduced, and this model was the first Trans-oceanic to feature FM. It was a greatly sought-after prize in the WPBFC's annual membership contest. (Courtesy Tim Smith.)

RADIO PERMIT. The Federal Communications Commission (FCC) issued this permit for radio transmission to angler Grady Stearns in 1961. In those days, it was required to have a license to operate on a radiotelephone station. The reverse side of the permit lists rules and prohibitions. Prohibitions include "use of obscene, indecent, or profane language" and "superfluous, false, or deceptive signals or communications." (Courtesy Grady Stearns.)

1959
UNITED STATES OF AMERICA
FEDERAL COMMUNICATIONS COMMISSION

RESTRICTED RADIOTELEPHONE OPERATOR PERMIT

This Permit, when countersigned by the permittee, authorizes

GRADY CARL STEARNS

to operate licensed radiotelephone stations for which this Permit is valid under Rules and Regulations of the Commission and for the life-time of the holder subject to suspension pursuant to the provisions of Section 303(m)(1) of the Communications Act and the Commission's Rules and Regulations.

FEDERAL COMMUNICATIONS COMMISSION

MAY   0 1961

Mary Jane Morris,
Secretary.

MIAMI, FLA.   RP-   7F9919

ISSUING OFFICER   SIGNATURE OF PERMITTEE

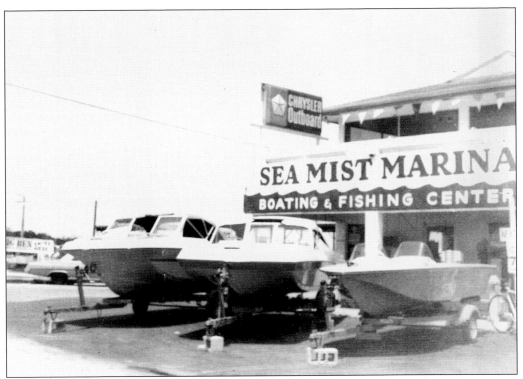

BOATING AND FISHING CENTER. This 1970s photograph shows the Sea Mist Marina Boating and Fishing Center in Boynton Beach. Throughout Palm Beach County, most marinas had a gas pump for selling fuel and often a little tackle store for bait, ice, and snacks. (Courtesy Janet Hall.)

LET'S GO FISHING. Here is an inside view of the Sea Mist Marina Boating and Fishing Center. An unknown lady holds a fishing pole that has a fish dangling from it. Fishing nets, rods, reels, and sundry items are on display. A sign for the *Sea Mist II* indicates the counter where one would buy tickets for drift fishing trips. (Courtesy Janet Hall.)

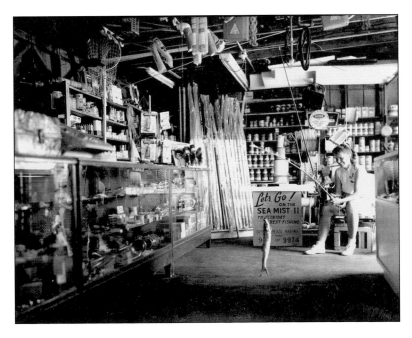

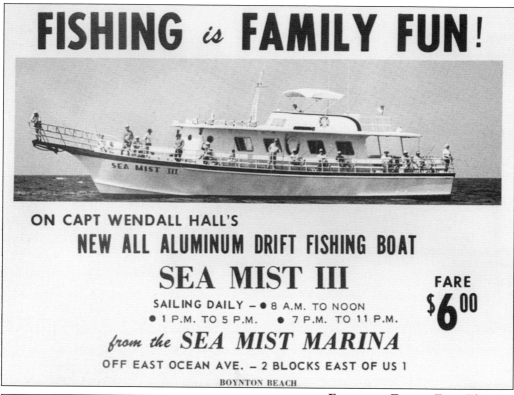

FISHING is FAMILY FUN!

ON CAPT WENDALL HALL'S

NEW ALL ALUMINUM DRIFT FISHING BOAT

SEA MIST III

SAILING DAILY – ● 8 A.M. TO NOON
● 1 P.M. TO 5 P.M. ● 7 P.M. TO 11 P.M.

from the **SEA MIST MARINA**

OFF EAST OCEAN AVE. – 2 BLOCKS EAST OF US 1

BOYNTON BEACH

FARE
$6.00

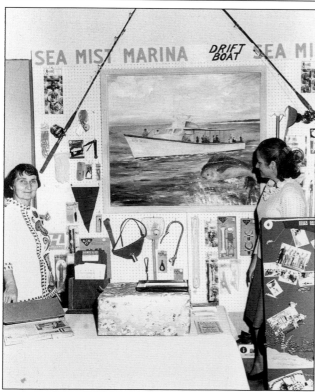

FISHING IS FAMILY FUN. This advertisement for Capt. Wendall Hall's new *Sea Mist III* is from the early 1970s. The newest drift fishing boat was all aluminum. The new fare for a four-hour trip was $6. (Courtesy Janet Hall.)

CHAMBER OF COMMERCE BOOTH. Janet Hall (left) and an unidentified young lady are shown with a fishing display at a Boynton Beach Chamber of Commerce event. The booth has an assortment of pennants, rods and reels, hooks, and other fishing accessories. (Courtesy Janet Hall.)

84

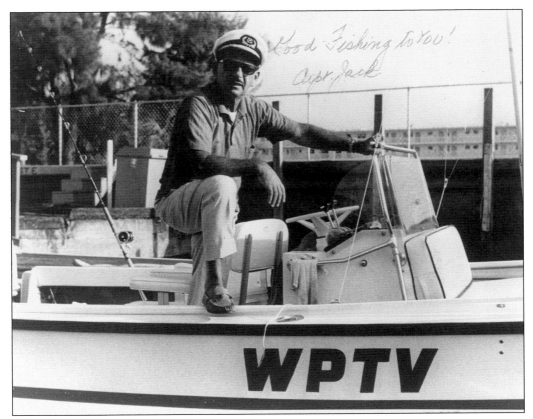

Good Fishing to You!
Capt. Jack

CAPT. JACK SMITH. Capt. Jack Smith moved to Florida from New Jersey in 1950 and had a half-hour live radio broadcast. Captain Jack was also famous for his daily *Five on 5* evening television fishing program. In addition, he was a fishing columnist for the *Delray News* and the *Lake Worth Herald*. Prior to coming to Florida, Captain Jack had been a professional boxer, a charter boat captain, and a lure manufacturer. The Captain Jack show was sponsored in part by Pepsi-Cola. To the delight of the viewers, Jack's bird (right) loved to drink Pepsi. (Courtesy WPBFC.)

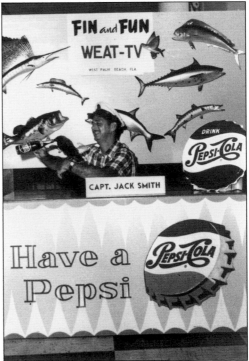

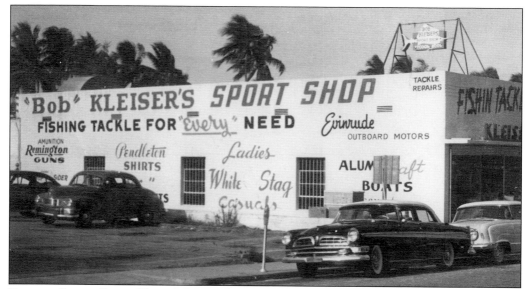

FAMOUS SPORT SHOP. Kleiser's Sport Shop was owned and operated by native Floridian Bob Kleiser. Bob graduated from Palm Beach High School and was past president of the WPBFC. This building, located at 125 Datura Street in West Palm Beach, was constructed in 1939. The original store had tiny aisles. They sold Tycoon rods and all types of sport fishing and hunting equipment. Kleiser would buy in volume from dealers and kept a full inventory. Consequently, sportsmen from all over the Palm Beaches came in to buy supplies, big game fishing tackle, and hunting equipment. (Courtesy Dan Kleiser.)

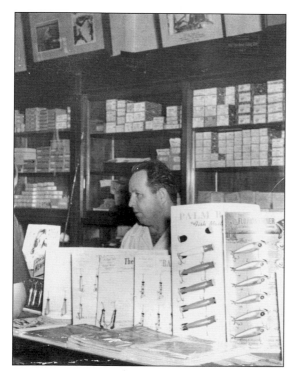

KLEISER'S SPORT SHOP. Owner Bob Kleiser, shown here, operated his sport fishing stores from 1934 to 1978. When he passed way, his son Dan took over and ran the store for another 20 years. (Courtesy Dan Kleiser.)

Seven

WEST PALM BEACH FISHING CLUB

ONE OF AMERICA'S GREATEST FISHING CLUBS. The WPBFC, founded in 1934 amidst the Great Depression, is one of the largest and oldest fishing clubs in the United States. The first club president, Cecil "Zeke" Cornelius, who was also a Palm Beach County commissioner, is the man on the right. The club was formed at the beginning of offshore fishing in the 1930s, when South Florida was a growing frontier. Community leaders saw the potential of sport fishing and the likelihood of the Palm Beaches becoming one of the world's top fishing destinations. (Courtesy WPBFC.)

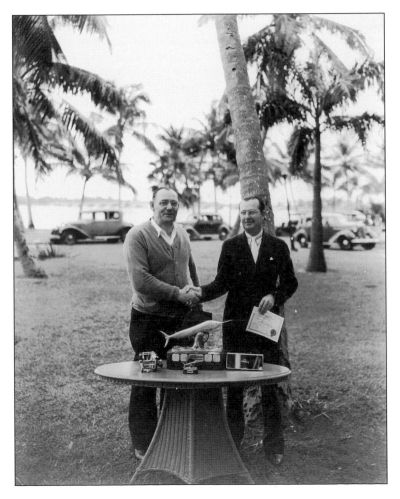

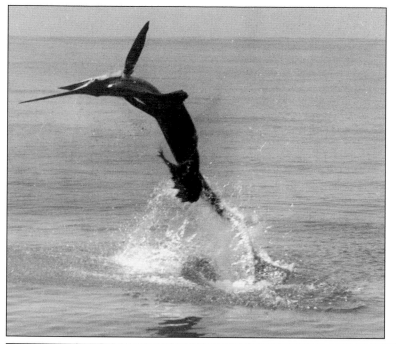

LEAPING SAILFISH. The outstanding sport fishing event, the annual Silver Sailfish Derby, was established in 1935. The event is the oldest running billfish tournament in the country, perhaps even the world. Here a silvery-blue sailfish, the mighty warrior of the Gulf Stream, leaps from the water. Sails are graceful and spectacular in action. The fish is well deserving of freedom after the fight is won. (Courtesy WPBFC.)

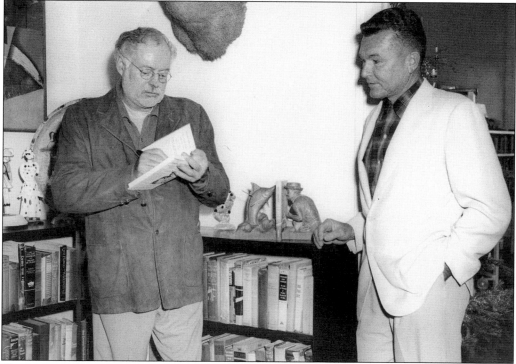

HEMINGWAY CONNECTION. Ernest Hemingway signs an edition of his novel *The Old Man and the Sea* that was presented to WPBFC president John Rybovich Jr. as part of the first Silver Sailfish Derby awards. The classic novel and a pair of the hand-carved wooden bookends shown in the background later became the annual award for the Master's Angling Tournament. This 1956 photograph was taken at Hemingway's country home near Havana, Cuba. (Courtesy WPBFC.)

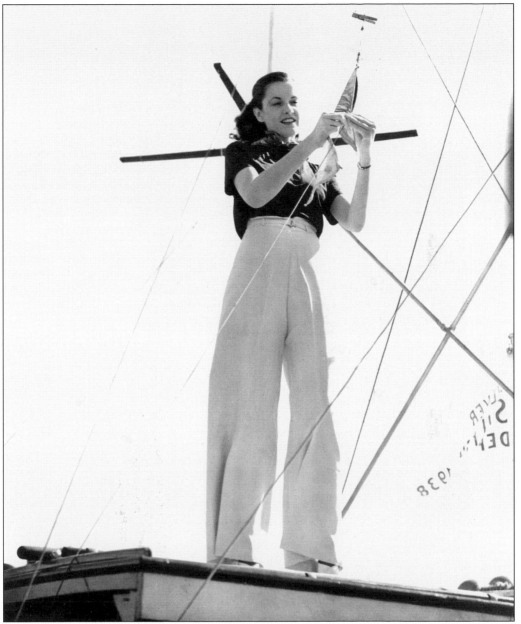

BIRTH OF THE RED RELEASE PENNANTS. Recognizing the need for conservation early, the WPBFC developed the red release sailfish flag so that crews could display the success of the day without putting all their fish on the dock. This practice is now recognized throughout the world. Here Marjorie Collins of West Palm Beach prepares to hoist two release pennants. The photograph was snapped during the 1938 Silver Sailfish Derby. (Courtesy WPBFC.)

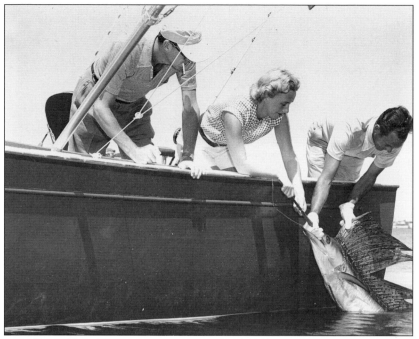

COOPERATIVE GAME FISH TAGGING PROGRAMS. In 1955, the University of Miami contacted the fishing club to help develop a tagging device for billfish (shown here) to study migratory behavior. The original tags were thick rubber bands meant to be slipped over the bills. This method was unsuccessful, and later a metal dart tag was developed by Floy Tag Company and the Woods Hole Oceanographic Institution. The project manager was scientist and author Frank Mather, a longtime WPBFC member. Hundreds of other members participated, and tens of thousands of billfish and tuna have been tagged and released from the 1960s to the present day. (Courtesy WPBFC.)

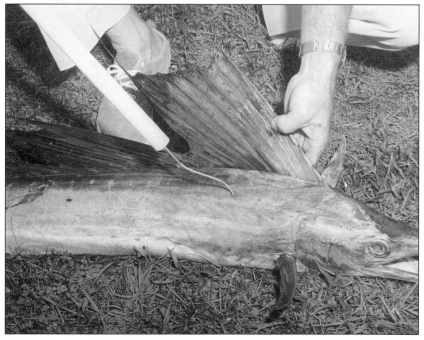

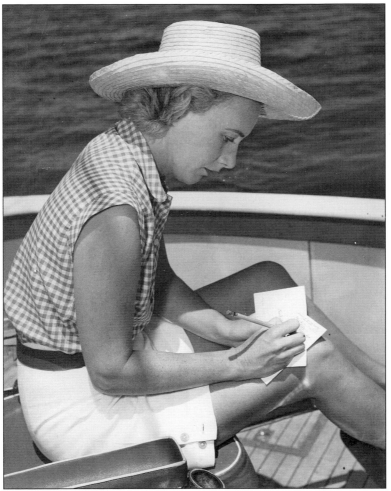

SUPPORTING SCIENCE. Mrs. Thomas Sheehan is filling out a tag release card for Woods Hole. John W. Jolley, president of the WPBFC as of 2008, was a marine biologist with the Florida Department of Natural Resources Marine Research Laboratory in St. Petersburg. In the early 1970s, the young marine expert set up a field laboratory and headquarters in the WPBFC office. The goal was to define biological parameters affecting the status of billfish, primarily sailfish, in the western North Atlantic. Today the National Marine Fisheries Service and the Billfish Foundation oversee the tagging program. The information, developed over time, is used to manage sailfish and other western North Atlantic billfish. (Courtesy WPBFC.)

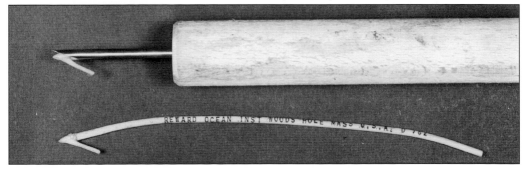

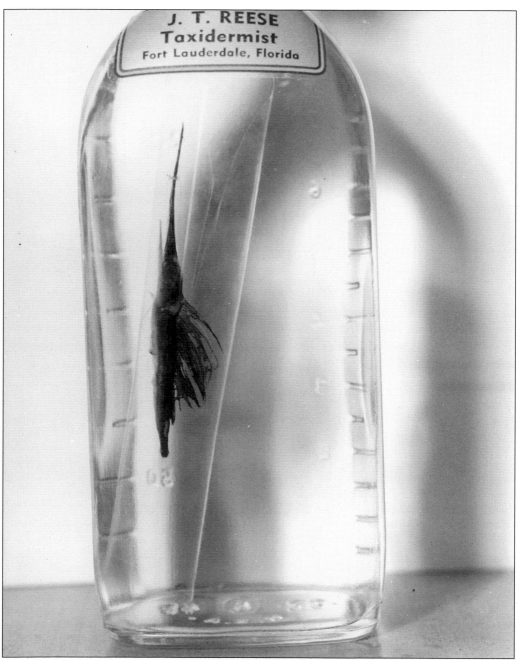

SAILFISH BIOLOGY. Because the sailfish had to be checked within several days of being caught, many WPBFC members helped with the study over the years. Al Pfleuger and J. T. Reese, area taxidermists, would call scientist John Jolley at the lab when they had fresh specimens. This is a juvenile sailfish about one month old. (Courtesy WPBFC.)

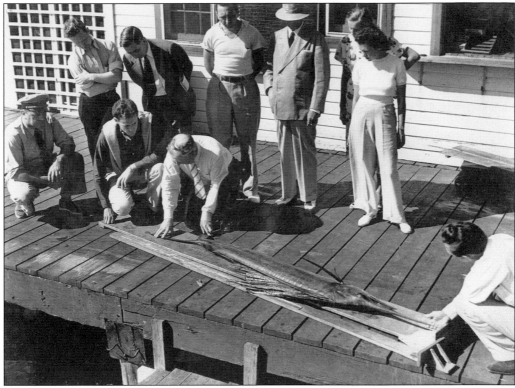

MEASURING BOARD. Fred C. N. Parke, entry official of the WPBFC (at center, kneeling), checks the length of a top trophy winner during a 1950s Silver Sailfish Derby at Anne's Dock in Palm Beach. Angler Sam Sprott of Stockbridge, Massachusetts, looks on as Parke pulls the tail fin out on the measuring board. The "gold button" sail measured 8 feet, 5-and-a-half inches long. (Courtesy WPBFC.)

SAILFISH CONSERVATION CLUB. This silver butane lighter award is inscribed with the words "Sailfish Conservation Club—The Palm Beaches." The Sailfish Conservation Club was formed by the WPBFC in the late 1930s. (Courtesy WPBFC.)

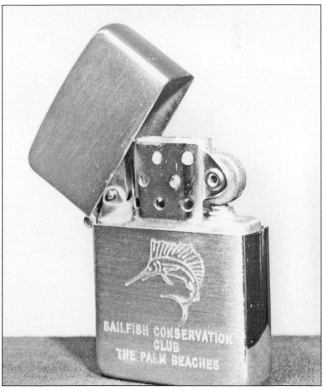

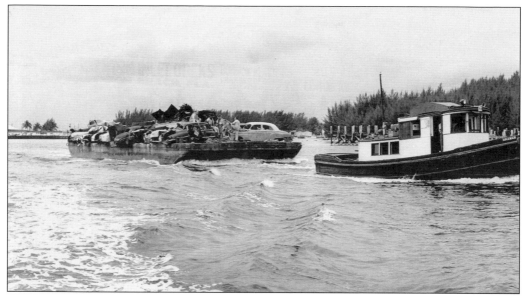

FLORIDA'S FIRST ARTIFICIAL REEF. The WPBFC sought out and received a permit in 1960 to start the first officially permitted artificial reef. The Palm Beach County government, the WPBFC, and John Rybovich planned the reef to enhance fishing. Three hundred automobiles, shown here, were dumped off a barge. Later the sinking of automobiles was discontinued because the metal deteriorates too quickly. The program is now directed by the Palm Beach County Department of Environmental Resources Management. Materials used today include old ships, concrete, and rock rubble. The new reefs attract fish and provide needed habitat. Snorkelers and scuba divers exploring the underwater reefs annually provide economic benefit to Palm Beach County. (Courtesy WPBFC.)

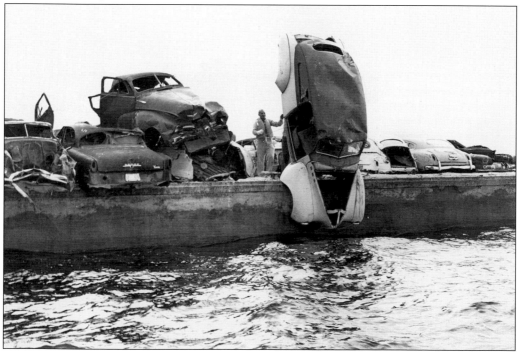

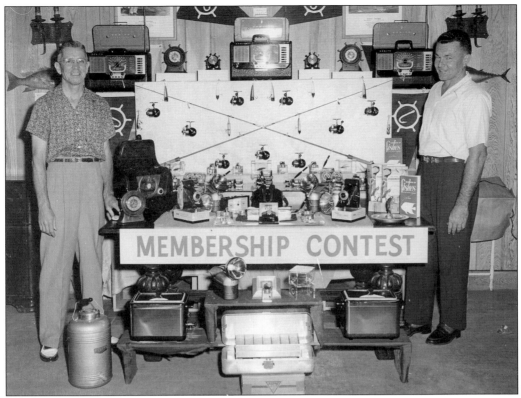

MEMBERSHIP CONTEST. The WPBFC Membership Committee chairman Myron Tedder (left) and club president John Rybovich are shown with prizes donated by fishing businesses that are awarded each year to club members who caught the biggest fish of each species. Later Tedder would become club president. (Courtesy WPBFC.)

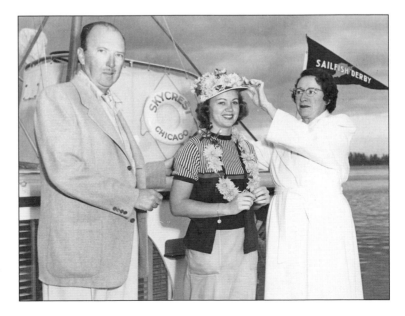

QUEEN OF THE DERBY. This photograph is of Marjorie Collins, Miss Sailfish Derby 1953. (Courtesy WPBFC.)

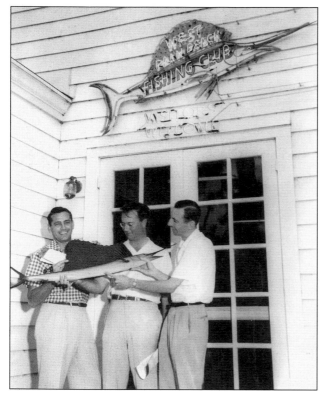

SAILFISH IS KING. Several members stand outside the WPBFC holding a small sailfish. Notice that the neon sign above the clubhouse doorway is a sailfish of similar proportions. (Courtesy WPBFC.)

CLUB ARCHIVE. The WPBFC has an extensive archive documenting local angling history. In addition to photographs, the collection includes tournament posters, trophies, pennants, and fishing memorabilia. Currently angling historian Michael Rivkin is writing a book detailing the WPBFC's glorious 75-year history, due out in 2009. (Courtesy WPBFC.)

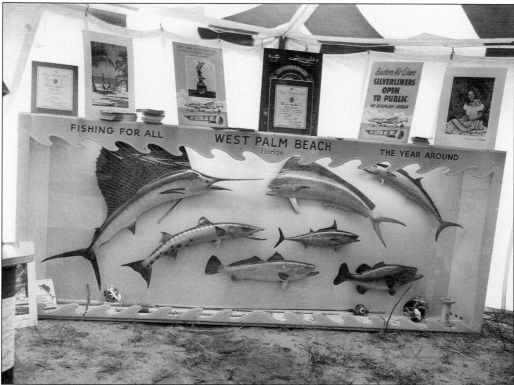

Eight

CAPTAINS AND CATCHES

CAPT. FRANK ARDINE. Palm Beach County has hundreds of well-respected charter boat captains. It would take an entire book to highlight each of them, but first of the local legends in this chapter is Capt. Frank Ardine (kneeling, at left) at Old Layton's Park Marina in Riviera Beach. Posing with him and the blue marlin are A. C. Scott (standing, left) and George Alger (standing, right) of Alger Trucking. More than 600 species of fish can be found in the Atlantic within a few miles of the Palm Beaches. (Courtesy WPBFC.)

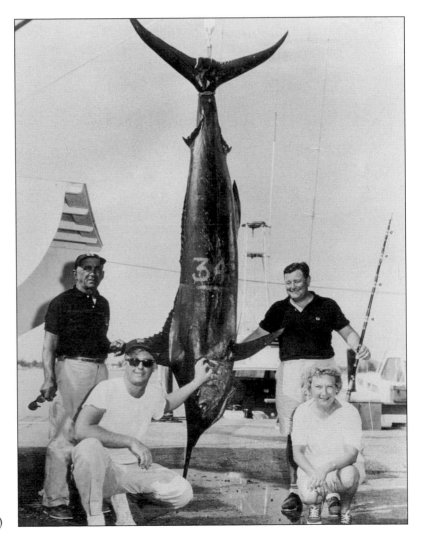

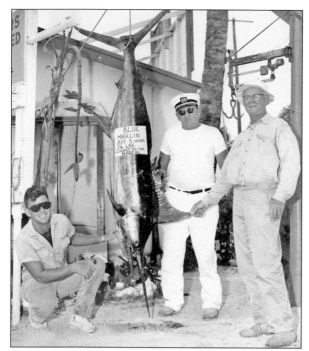

CAPT. JACK WILLIAMS. The blue marlin caught aboard Jack Williams's boat, the *Rascal*, tipped the Chastillion scales at 116 pounds. The *Rascal* was named after Captain Williams's bull terrier dog. Jack, one of the earliest charter boat captains in the south end of the county, was a mentor to other local captains. When the Boynton Inlet was especially treacherous, Jack stood in the pump house watching the waves, his visuals and directions helping guide the boats into the inland waterway. His mate, Jim, is on the left, and an unidentified angler is at right. (Courtesy Williams family.)

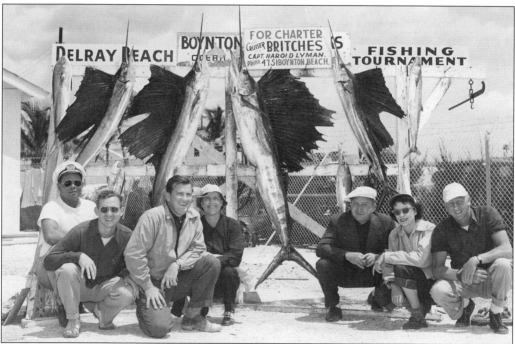

CAPT. "BUDDY" MOORE. Moore started as a "striker," or mate, on charter fishing boats in the late 1940s. He worked with local boat captains and put himself through medical school. He became a surgeon and noted figure in the development of many local hospitals in Palm Beach County. Dr. Moore was also the first doctor to develop and start the Emergency Medical Technician program in the United States. He is on the right, and Capt. Harold Lyman is on the left. (Courtesy Charles Moore.)

CAPT. BOB HAINES. Haines (left) and Capt. Jackie Morrow (right) pose with owners of the *Lovango III*, Mr. and Mrs. Henry Minis of Savannah, Georgia, at Bill's Sailfish Marina in the late 1960s. The pair of blue marlin was caught off Palm Beach with 80-pound tackle and on rigged black mullet. (Courtesy Bill Buckland's Fisherman's Charter.)

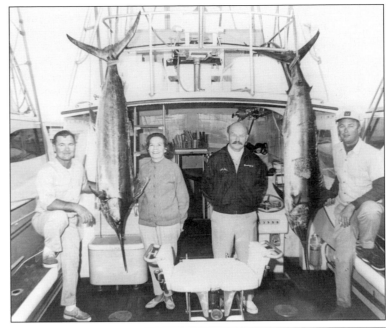

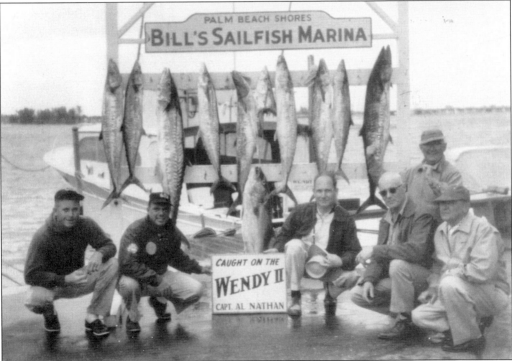

CAPT. AL NATHAN. This picture taken at Bill's Sailfish Marina in Palm Beach Shores shows legendary Capt. Al Nathan (left, with his hand on the sign) posing with a fishing party. The late Al Nathan was a lifetime WPBFC member and supported many club and foundation programs over the years. A Capt. Al Nathan Memorial Scholarship was established to aid graduate students involved with the marine sciences at Florida Atlantic University's Charles E. Schmidt College of Science. (Courtesy WPBFC Archives.)

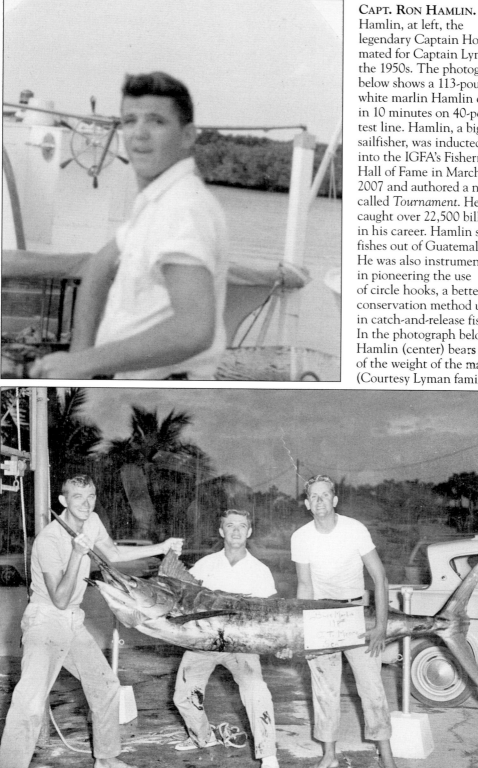

CAPT. RON HAMLIN. Hamlin, at left, the legendary Captain Hook, mated for Captain Lyman in the 1950s. The photograph below shows a 113-pound white marlin Hamlin caught in 10 minutes on 40-pound test line. Hamlin, a big-time sailfisher, was inducted into the IGFA's Fisherman's Hall of Fame in March 2007 and authored a novel called *Tournament*. He has caught over 22,500 billfish in his career. Hamlin still fishes out of Guatemala. He was also instrumental in pioneering the use of circle hooks, a better conservation method used in catch-and-release fishing. In the photograph below, Hamlin (center) bears most of the weight of the marlin. (Courtesy Lyman family.)

CAPT. JANET GARNSEY HALL. Hall came to Florida in 1923 and as a young woman worked as a diver/entertainer on a glass-bottom boat in Fort Lauderdale. Not content to dive for shells and wave to the crowd, she started running the boat when she was 22 years old. When the Coast Guard required boat operators to be licensed, Janet took the captain's test and was awarded her license. She was the only licensed female boat captain in Palm Beach County for many years. (Courtesy Janet Hall.)

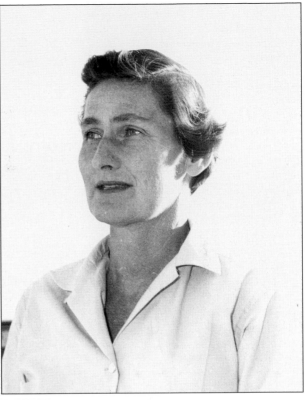

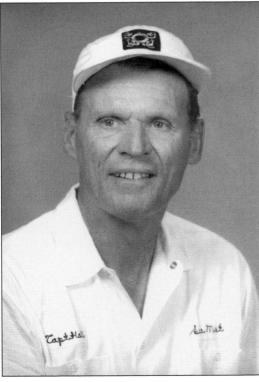

CAPT. WENDALL HALL. Hall was the co-owner/operator of the Sea Mist Marina with his wife, Janet. The pair was one of the only husband/wife teams of boat captains in the area for many years. (Courtesy Janet Hall.)

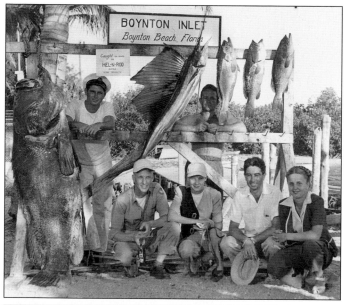

CAPT. HERB SCHULZ. Schulz skippered his first charter boat in 1939 when he was just 16 years old. He served in the navy during World War II and has rescued dozens of people at sea during his 60 years as a charter boat captain. In this photograph, Captain Schulz is seen to the left with a goliath grouper. Hanging from the fish board are several grey grouper, commonly caught in 80 to 90 feet of water off the Gulf Stream Clubhouse. Schulz's son John owns and manages the tackle shop at the Lady-K Dock in Lantana. (Courtesy John Schulz.)

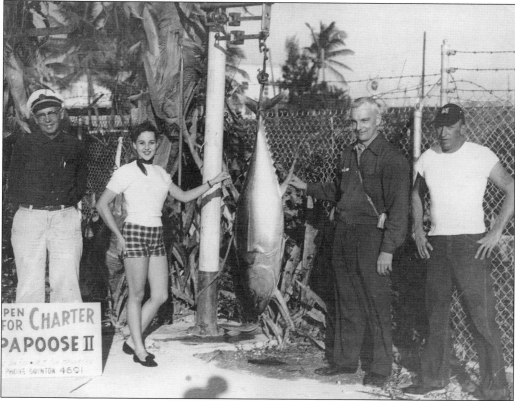

CAPT. VAN EPP. Van Epp was a pioneer in the sport fishing industry. He found prime fishing spots and remembered them by watching and observing. He practiced triangulation using landmarks such as the Boynton Casino, the water tower, and the Lake Worth Pier as reference points. Van Epp is on the left with members of a fishing party and a yellowfin tuna. Mate Bob "Anteater" Hennigan is on the right. (Courtesy Donald Van Epp.)

CAPT. HOWARD LANCE. One of the early Palm Beach boat captains was Howard Lance. His boat *Cheerio* was based at the Royal Poinciana Dock in Palm Beach. Here he is between sons Jack and Bill. All three men were in the U.S. Navy in 1943. Jack and Bill became two of the most respected charter boat captains and later captained the boats of wealthy Palm Beach residents. (Courtesy Lance family.)

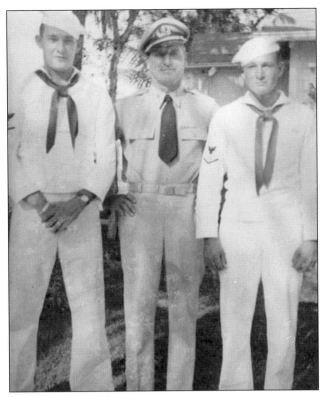

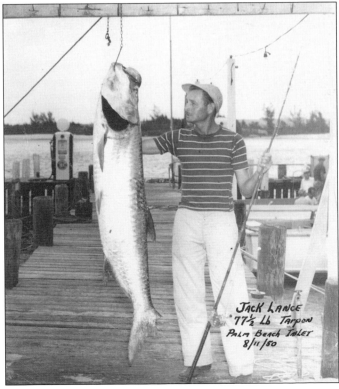

JACK LANCE
77½ Lb Tarpon
Palm Beach Inlet
8/11/50

CAPT. JACK LANCE. This image from 1950 shows Jack Lance holding a homemade Burma rod he used to catch this tarpon. Lance used an extra wide Shakespeare reel loaded with linen line to land the tarpon near Palm Beach Inlet. By the 1960s, Lance had switched to braided nylon line. (Courtesy WPBFC.)

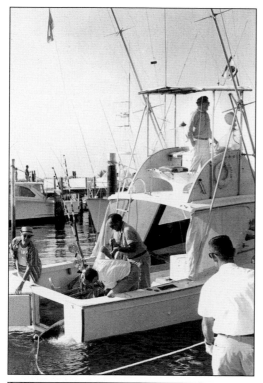

RARE CATCH. Dr. Jack "Doc" Liggett started fishing on the old Headley's Palm Beach Pier. His dad, Lester Liggett, ran the restaurant on the pier, and George DeBay operated the Sport Shop. In March 1964, Doc captured media attention while participating in the Buccaneer Yacht Club Blue Marlin Tournament on Singer Island along with Capt. Nels Applegate and mate Billy Lance. Doc boated a 244-pound blue marlin (below), and hours later that same day he pulled in a 382-pound bluefin tuna. The accomplishment is said to be the only bluefin and blue marlin ever caught in Palm Beach waters in a single day. In 1964, there was no limit to the size of the line in the Buccaneer Tournament. Doc said it took about 10 minutes to whip the marlin and about an hour and a half to wear down the tuna. As the big tuna came closer to the boat, mate Billy Lance yelled, "There's no bill on this one!" Everyone was surprised by the appearance of bluefin tuna in these waters. The incident earned Doc the nickname of "Lucky Liggett." (Courtesy Jack Liggett.)

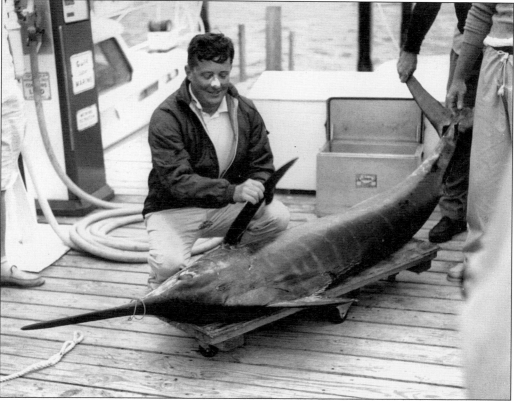

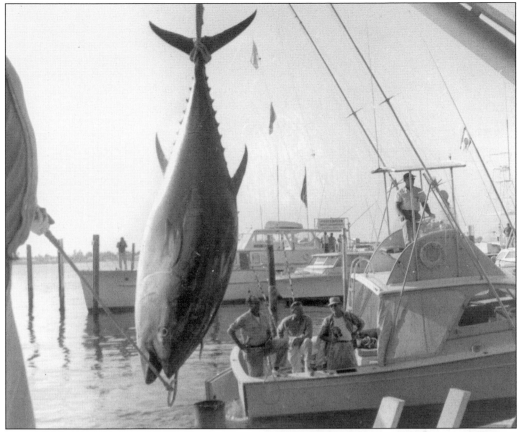

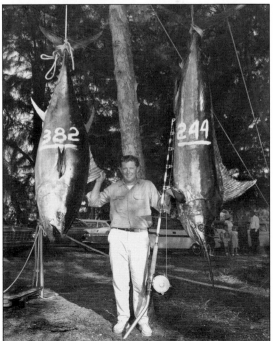

TUNA TIME. The bluefin tuna looks even larger than 382 pounds as in hangs in the foreground of the scene above. Notice the other tournament participants looking on from boats in the background; some are even snapping pictures. They almost sank the boat when they pulled the tuna in alongside the blue marlin. Angler Doc Liggett would learn he swept the awards in the Buccaneer Tourney by winning in four categories. According to published reports, the tourney had 62 anglers competing aboard 38 boats. In the photograph at right, Doc Liggett proudly stands between his record catches. This record will likely never be repeated. (Courtesy Jack Liggett.)

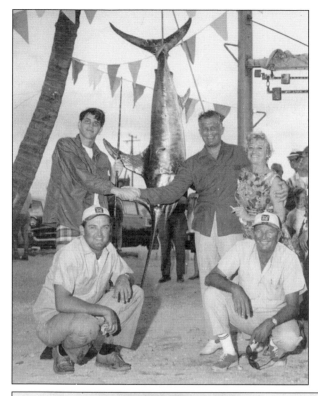

CAPT. FRED HASTINGS. Hastings (kneeling, right) and Capt. Jack Conners (kneeling, left) pose with a swordfish and unknown anglers at Sailfish Marina. (Courtesy Capt. Tim Smith.)

CAPT. KENNY LYMAN. Lyman (below, right), owner of Lyman's Sport Fishing Dock, returns with a happy fishing party and a mixed bag of fish. The Lyman family members were pioneers of Lantana and owned a store near the site of the current Lantana Bridge. The original Lyman homestead, built in 1893, is currently the home of a popular restaurant on the Intracoastal Waterway now called the Old Key Lime House. Kenny Lyman, a charter boat captain for over 40 years, enjoyed helping children land a big game fish. (Courtesy Lyman family.)

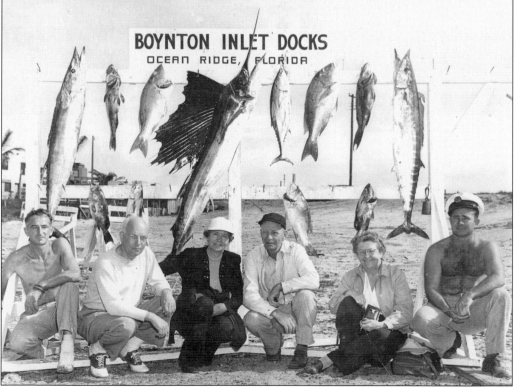

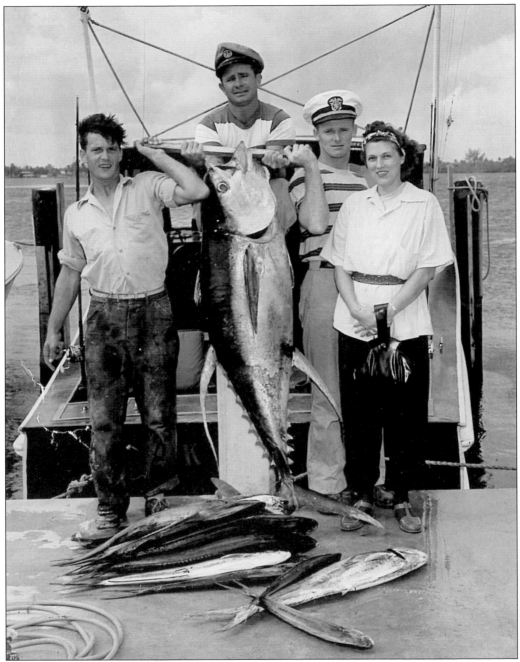

Capt. Red Waggener. Red was a Lake Worth native and a U.S. Navy pilot who flew Corsairs in World War II. After attending the University of Miami, Red was a charter boat captain for 40 years. He was also an expert woodcarver, creating art out of teak or maple. Here Red (with striped shirt and captain's hat) is helping Capt. Kenny Lyman (center) hold up a yellowfin tuna. Lester Williams is the mate on the left. The girl on the right is unidentified. (Courtesy Lyman family.)

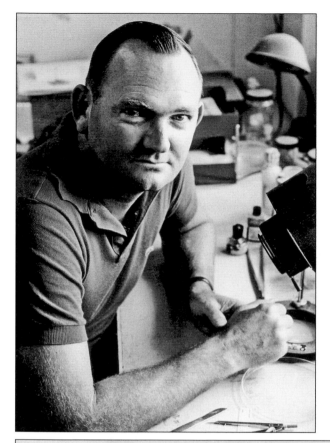

DR. GILBERT VOSS. Voss was from a Palm Beach County pioneer family. He grew up in Hypoluxo and attended the University of Miami, earning masters and doctorate degrees in marine biology. He was an authority on the life cycle of sailfish and pushed to preserve John Pennekamp State Park. According to Gilbert, "People are more interesting than fish and fishermen more interesting than most people." (Courtesy Rosenstiel School of Marine and Atmospheric Science Library, University of Miami)

BROTHERS VOSS. Gilbert's brothers, Frederick (left) and Walter (right), shown below with a barracuda, were also popular charter boat captains in Palm Beach and Broward Counties. The Voss brothers represent one of the oldest pioneer families in Palm Beach County. (Courtesy Marjorie Nelson.).

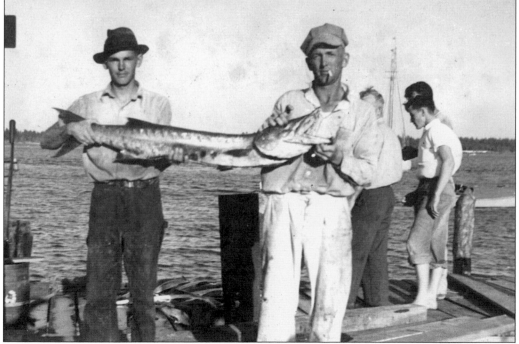

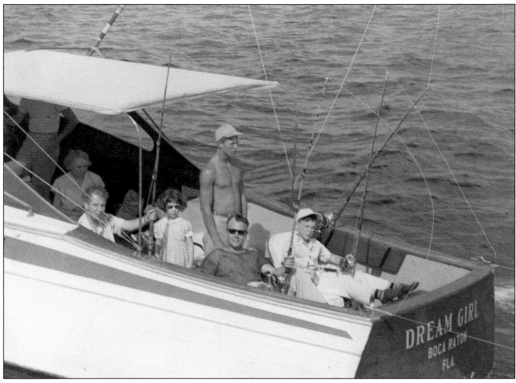

FISHING FAMILIES. *Dream Girl* was a sport fishing boat owned and operated by Capt. Walter Voss out of Boca Raton and Fort Lauderdale. In this 1948 photograph, Captain Voss's nephew Freddy is the mate, standing in the center of the boat. The original *Dream Girl* was a 36-foot Backus cabin sea skiff. (Courtesy Marjorie Nelson.)

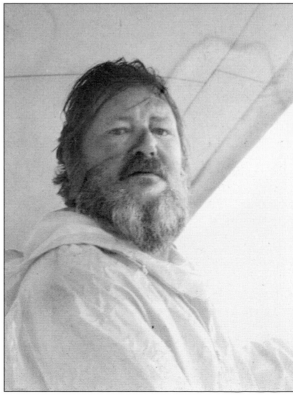

CAPT. FREDDY VOSS. Voss (shown here), the son of Frederick Voss, was said by many to be a character and one of the best fishermen of his era. (Courtesy Capt. Jimmy Duncan.)

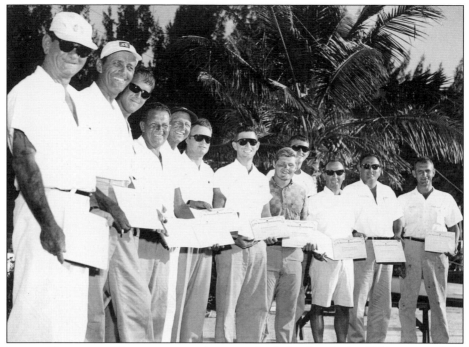

LIFESAVING CAPTAINS. The captains and mates who helped with the 1964 rescue of the *Two Georges* boat accident victims were honored by the American Red Cross with a special award. Local men are shown above with their certificates, and below is a copy of the certificate. (Courtesy Capt. Jimmy Duncan.)

+

The American National Red Cross

TO

JIMMIE DUNCAN

IN GRATEFUL APPRECIATION

FOR HEROIC SERVICES RENDERED ON MARCH 25, 1964 WHEN HE ASSISTED IN THE SWIMMING RESCUE OF VICTIMS OF THE BOAT ACCIDENT AT THE BOYNTON INLET, BOYNTON BEACH, FLORIDA.

CHAPTER

Palm Beach County Chapter

DATE

April 8, 1964

CHAIRMAN

B.D.Cole B.D.Cole

Ben York Ben York

Nine

DOCKS AND MARINAS

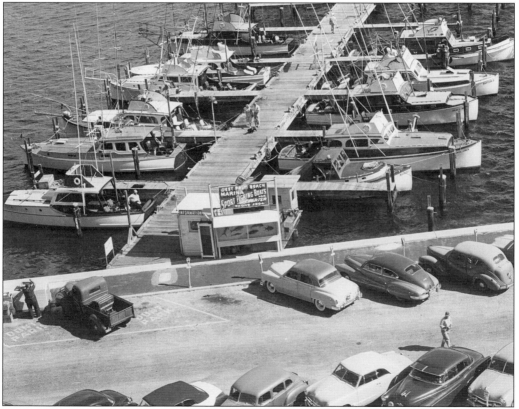

CITY DOCK. Sport fishing has been a popular pastime in the Palm Beaches since the 1870s. At the West Palm Beach Municipal Dock around 1953, many charter boats docked and took visitors angling for marlin, sailfish, kingfish, and Atlantic dolphin. The dock was situated across from the George Washington Hotel, now the Helen Wilkes Retirement Home. This location was close to hotels and the major shopping areas, and many winter visitors booked charters from here. (Courtesy Vern Pickup Crawford.)

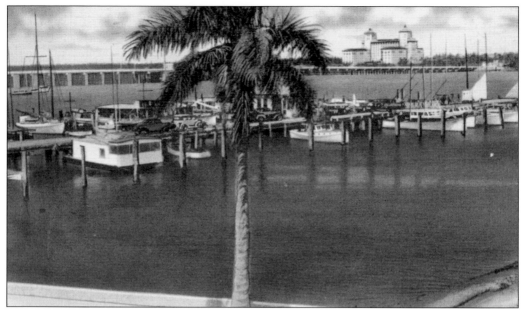

PALM BEACH YACHT BASIN. This 1940s postcard view shows the Palm Beach Yacht Basin. It was home to the *Orca*, from which presidents Hoover and Franklin Roosevelt enjoyed sailfishing. (Courtesy Capt. Tim Smith.)

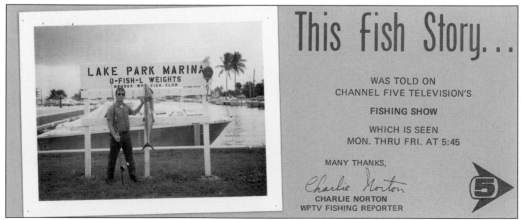

LAKE PARK MARINA. John Jolley poses in front of the scales with a kingfish at the Lake Park Marina, which still stands today, expanded and improved. The marina was an official WPBFC weigh station. John appeared on the *Fishing Show* with WPTV Channel Five fishing reporter Charlie Norton. This image of John and the kingfish he caught on light tackle for the WPBFC Tournament was a souvenir from the day. (Courtesy John Jolley.)

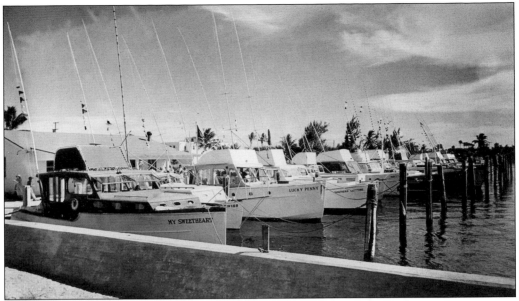

BOYNTON INLET DOCKS. In the early 1950s, the bustling Boynton Inlet Docks were home to over 20 charter boats. South Lake Worth's Boynton Inlet is not a natural inlet but was dug in 1926. Many people consider the inlet very treacherous. To this day, the U.S. Coast Guard does not consider it to be a navigable inlet. Some of the boats seen in this photograph are *My Sweetheart, Lucky Penny, Southern Comfort,* and *Papoose.* (Courtesy Dr. Charles Moore.)

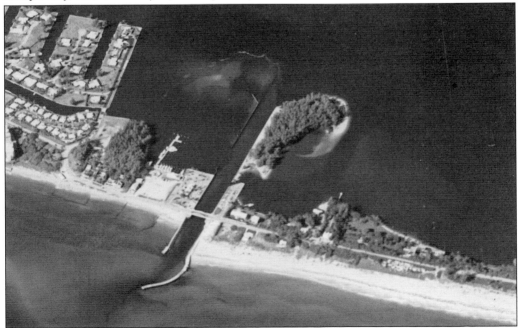

SOUTH LAKE WORTH INLET. This view shows the inlet, known by locals as Boynton Inlet, from above. Boynton Beach is know as the "Gateway to the Gulf Stream," because anglers can be in 100 feet of water in just a few minutes via the inlet. The small island in the center of the picture was known as Beer Can Island. Today the island is a bird sanctuary designated by the Audubon Society and called Bird Island. (Courtesy Boynton Beach City Library Archives.)

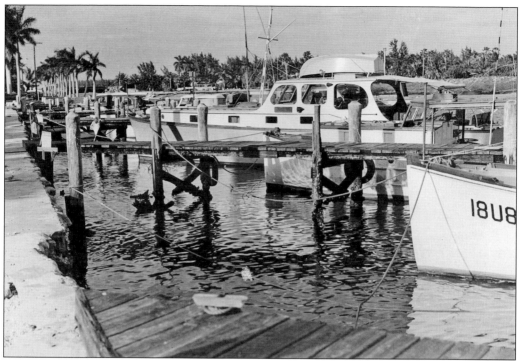

BOYNTON BEACH YACHT BASIN. These private boat accommodations were known as the Boynton Beach Yacht Basin. The docks were located behind the Howard Johnson's at Ocean Avenue and Dixie (now Federal) Highway in Boynton Beach. (Courtesy Capt. Jack Williams family.)

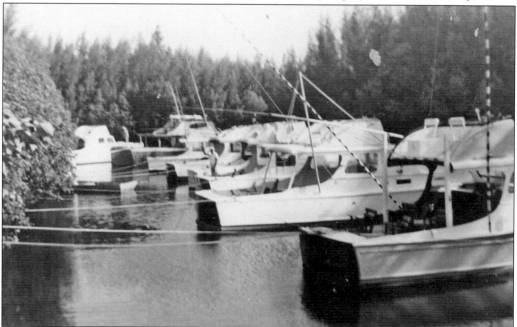

HURRICANE HOLE. This harbor, known as "Hurricane Hole" or "Spanish Cove," was along the Intracoastal Waterway in Ocean Ridge just south of where the harbor development is today. The photograph is dated 1960. (Courtesy Capt. Jack Williams family.)

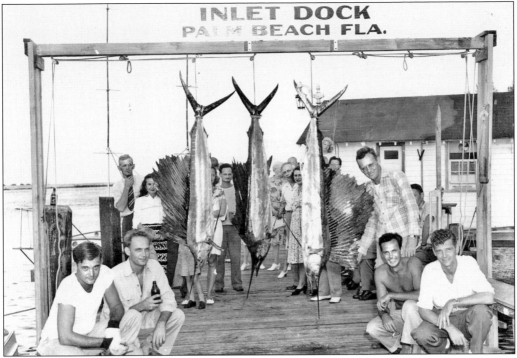

INLET DOCK'S PALM BEACH. A large group of anglers and spectators pose with these billfish on one of the most popular docks in Palm Beach County's history. (Courtesy Lance family.)

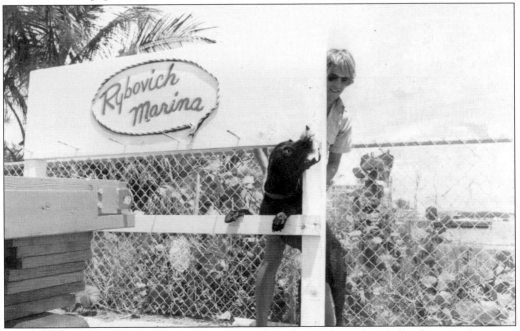

RYBOVICH MARINA. Danny Shea and his black lab Archie peek out from behind a sign advertising the Rybovich Marina. The famous boatyard and marina used to be in West Palm Beach. Captain Shea worked for Mel Spencer and John Rybovich at Spencer's boatyard and the Rybovich boatyard in the 1960s and 1970s. (Courtesy of Capt. Danny Shea.)

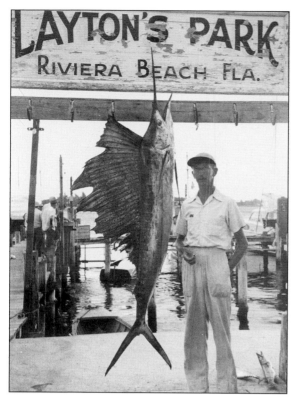

LAYTON'S PARK. The docks at Layton's mobile home park were a popular place for charter boats until it closed around 1961. It was located directly across from the Palm Beach Inlet. After Layton's closed, the charter boatmen moved to Bill's Dock or the Sailfish Center, which was closer to the inlet. (Courtesy Vern Pickup Crawford.)

BILL'S DOCK. The popular Sailfish Marina was started by Bill Bachstet in 1957 and was known simply as Bill's Dock. Bachstet rented small boats and built some slips large enough for charter boats. The original occupants were Frank Ardine's *Sail Ahoy*, Bob Rast's *Comanche*, Al Nathan's *Wendy II*, and Johnny Thomas's *Joker*. In this vintage photograph, a lady angler shows off her nice catch. (Courtesy WPBFC.)

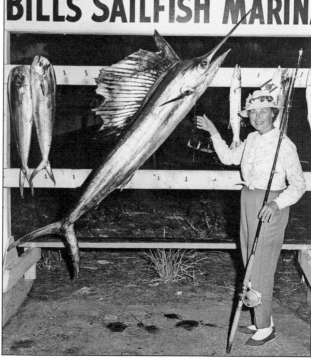

Ten

THE TRADITIONS CONTINUE

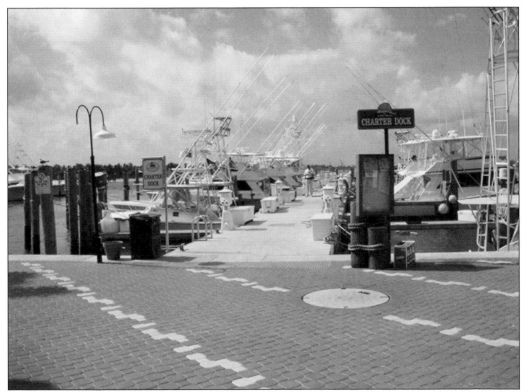

BEAUTIFUL SAILFISH MARINA. This is the charter dock at beautiful Sailfish Marina. Due to conservation awareness and efforts over the years, Palm Beach County is still a wonderful place to live, boat, and fish. Time, heavy fishing, and pollution may have changed our estuaries and reefs, but biologists say the marine life is coming back. Today more anglers own their own boats, and there are fewer charter and drift boats per capita compared to the early days. The sport fishing industry is a boon to Palm Beach County, and through education and awareness, many time-honored traditions continue into the 21st century. (Courtesy Janet DeVries.)

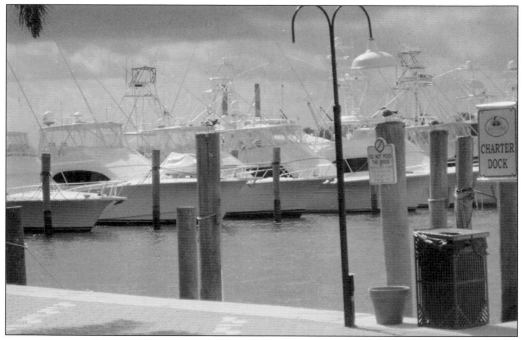

SPORT FISHING BOATS. Charter sport fishing boats line up at the Sailfish Marina. Some of the boats and captains docking here in 2008 include Capt. Bill Davis, with *Anejo*; Capt. Steve Rea, with *Black Duck*; Capt. John Krohn, with *Boomerang*; Capt. Kip Edwards, with *Fighting Lady*; Capt. Chris Recchio, with *Fish With Me*; Capt. Tim Dillon, with *Island Clan*; Capt. Howie Vermilye, with *LaVida*; Capt. Matt Rabenstine, with *Miss Annie*; Capt. Mark Terpeney, with *No Frills*; Capt. Joe Drosey, with *Rhonda's Osprey*; and Capt. Tony Rizzo, with *Thumper*. (Courtesy Janet DeVries.)

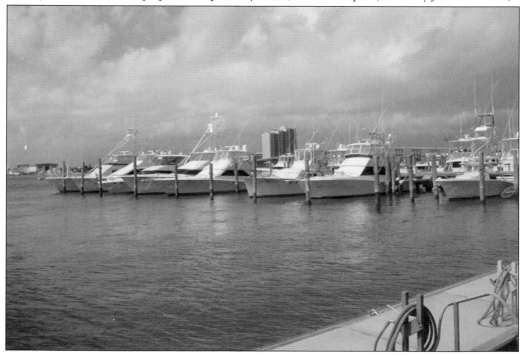

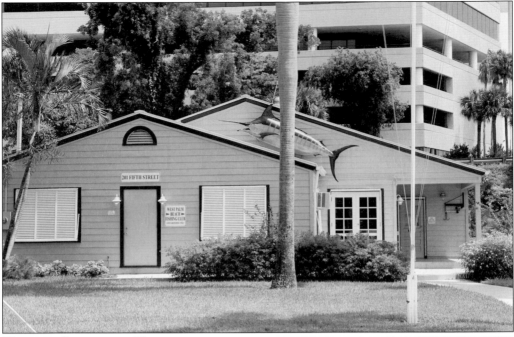

HISTORIC CLUBHOUSE. The current WPBFC clubhouse on North Flagler Drive and Fifth Street in West Palm Beach was built in 1941, several years after the club was formed. Inside the building are original skin mounts of several dozen billfish, bottom fish, and reef fish. Photographs, trophies, fishing antiques, and memorabilia line the walls. In 2007, the club had approximately 1,400 members. (Courtesy Steve Anton.)

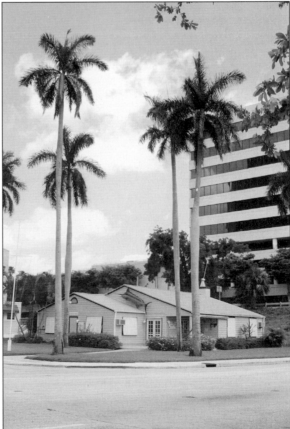

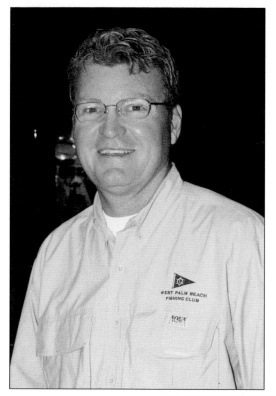

TOM TWYFORD. Twyford has served as executive director of the WPBFC since 1988. During his tenure, the club has grown by nearly 200 members, and the club is no longer in debt. Some of the many exciting annual events including a summer fishing contest, winter fishing contest, Silver Sailfish Derby, marine yard sale, Everglades National Park outing, PBC KDW Classic, Bahamas outing, Indian River Lagoon outing, Kids' Fishing Day program, volunteer appreciation party and fish fry, and a barbecue and auction. The club is dedicated to conservation. (Courtesy Steve Anton.)

IWFA TODAY. This 2007 photograph is of, from left to right, Cindy Lyman Jamison and author Janet DeVries with International Women's Fishing Association cofounder Kay Rybovich and current IWFA president Gwen Hahn at the beautiful Sailfish Club of Florida. Today the IWFA, housed in the International Game Fishing Association Museum, hosts tournaments all over the world and has over 200 active members. (Courtesy Steve Anton.)

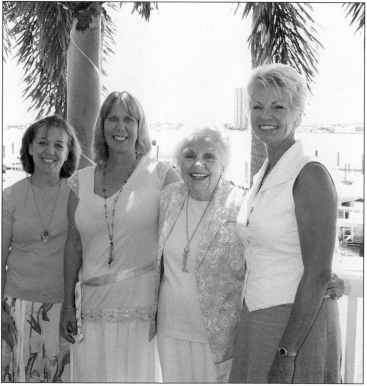

JOHN JOLLEY. Longtime WPBFC president John Jolley (center) pauses for a photograph on his 25-foot, custom-built Topaz *We Tag 'Em*. The name of the boat reflects the work John started as a marine biologist in the early 1970s, studying the life cycle of the sailfish. John has served as WPBFC president since 1982. His nephew Johnny is at left, and his brother Bob is at right. (Courtesy John Jolley.)

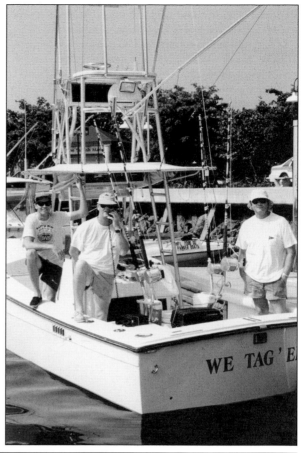

KIDS' FISHING DAY. The Palm Beach County Fishing Foundation is the charitable affiliate of the WPBFC. Since 1986, the foundation has held an annual Kids' Fishing Day program. Nearly 100 volunteers and thousands of sponsors combine efforts to provide youngsters who don't have the opportunity or the means to experience offshore fishing with a day of marine environmental education, angling instruction, and a deep-sea adventure. (Courtesy WPBFC.)

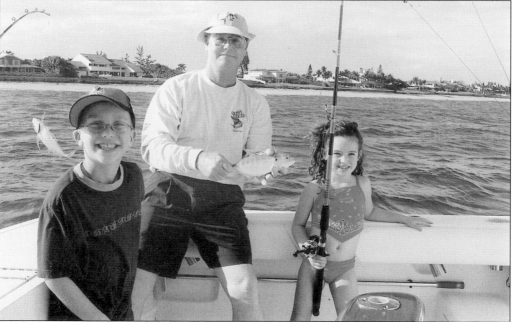

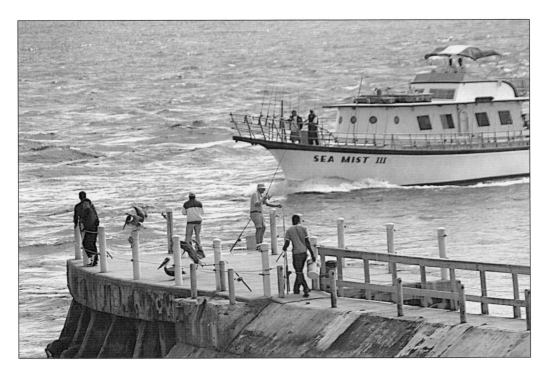

SEA MIST III. The *Sea Mist III*, a 65-foot all-aluminum boat designed to carry 61 passengers, was first launched in April 1972. The drift boat, shown in both of these photographs in 2008 heading into the Boynton Inlet, still takes passengers on daily fishing trips and is operated by the Garnsey family. (Courtesy Steve Anton.)

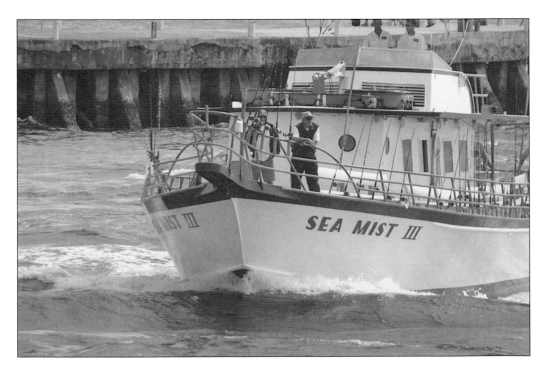

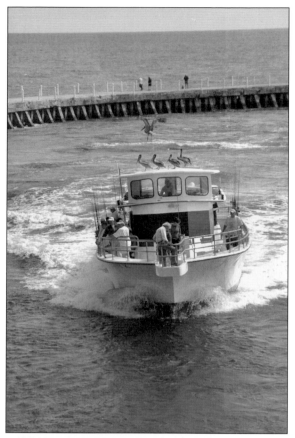

ON THE WATER. *Lady K*, part of the B-Love Fleet, navigates the Boynton Inlet. Boats like this one are used by the WPBFC in their annual Kids' Fishing Day event scheduled each August. (Courtesy Steve Anton.)

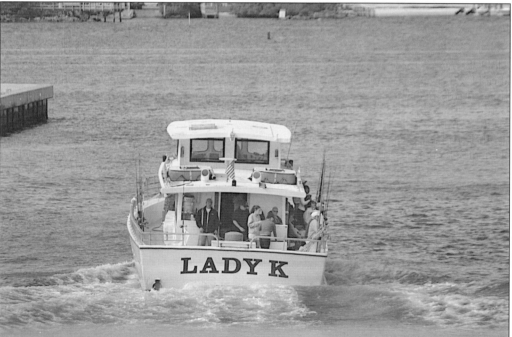

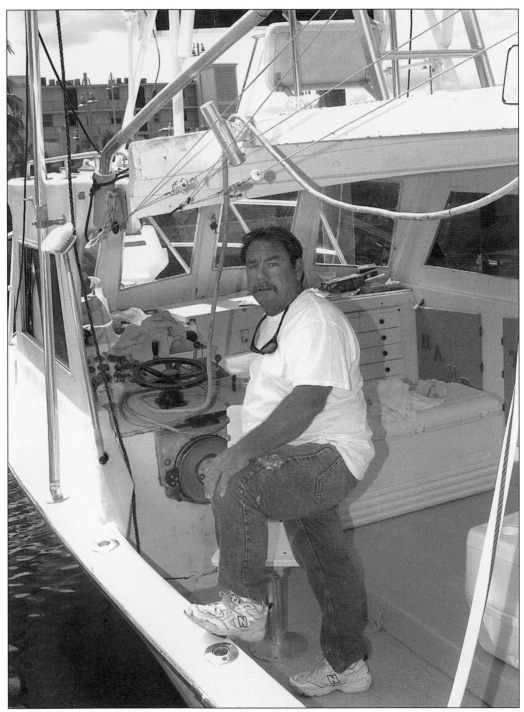

HAMR-TIME. Charter boat captain Paul Fasolo, a Boynton native, is one of a few longtime charter boat operators still making daily runs into the deep blue. His boat, *Hamr-Time*, shown here, has the last commercial fishing license out of the Boynton area, because Paul's boat was originally the *Breadwinner*, a lobster boat owned by Bill and Jean Dilcher. The boat has been converted into a sport fisher. (Courtesy Steve Anton.)

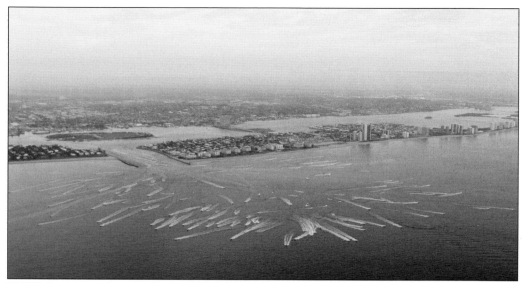

KDW Classic. The KDW Classic fishing tournament is hosted by the City of Riviera Beach and the WPBFC at the Riviera Beach Municipal Marina. The event is a fun, reasonably priced tournament that stimulates the local marine and fishing industry and benefits marine conservation and educational efforts of the WPBFC and its charitable affiliate. The Palm Beach County Fishing Foundation's annual Kids' Fishing Day for underprivileged and at-risk youth and Rods and Reels for Kids are two programs that benefit from tournament proceeds. (Courtesy WPBFC.)

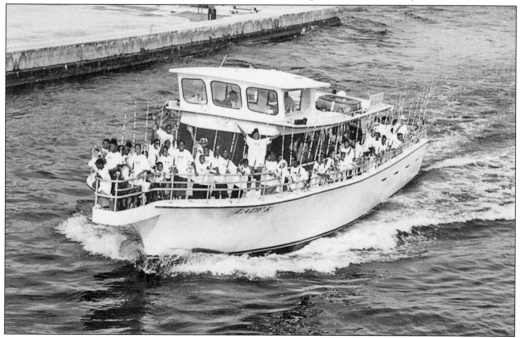

WPBFC Kids' Fishing Day. For over 20 years, the outreach program of the WPBFC has been an annual Kids' Fishing Day. The event targets children who normally don't have the opportunity or the means to experience offshore fishing aboard a big boat. The program also includes fishing techniques and boating safety. In this photograph, a happy group waves from the drift boat *Lady K.* (Courtesy WPBFC.)

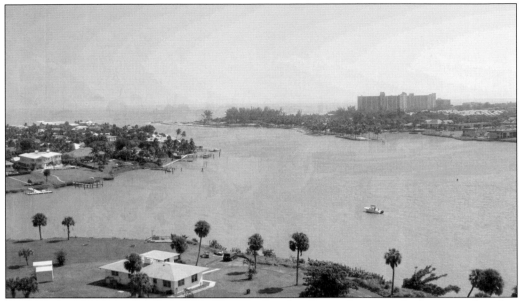

JUPITER INLET. Originally an outlet for the Loxahatchee River, this natural inlet was widened in 1967. The channel has been maintained over the years through periodic dredging of the "Sand Trap," the sand from which is placed downdrift of the inlet to combat beach erosion. (Courtesy Steve Anton.)

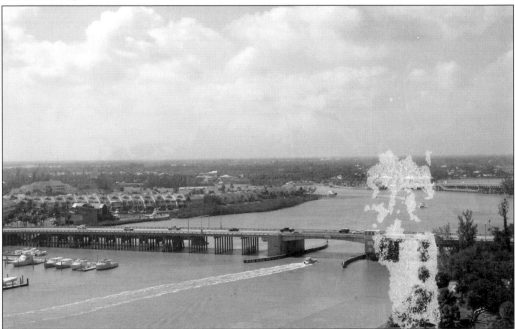

JUPITER LIGHTHOUSE. This inland waterway view was taken from the top of the Jupiter Inlet Lighthouse. First lit on July 10, 1860, it is the oldest existing structure in Palm Beach County. It was designed by George Meade, and in 1973, this lighthouse was put on the National Register of Historic Places. The lighthouse is an active maritime aid to navigation and is maintained by the U.S. Coast Guard. Before advanced navigational equipment, the lighthouse was used as a reference point for boats and fishermen. (Courtesy Steve Anton.)

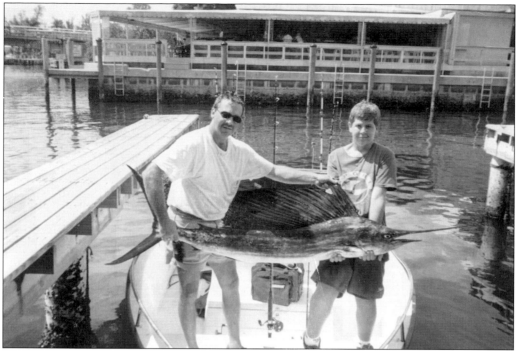

THE FUTURE. Longtime anglers know there is no better place than out on the water. Many people are drawn to the sea—there's something about being surrounded by the beauty of nature, the fresh air, and the anticipation of hooking the next "big one." The sense of adventure and the thrill of the catch keep people going back for more. As for the littlest anglers, they just know fishing is an outdoor sport, and it's fun. (Courtesy Steve Anton.)

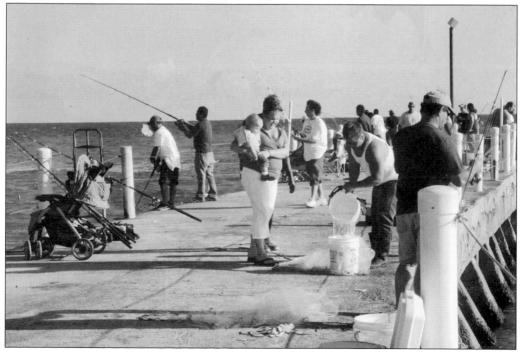

ACROSS AMERICA, PEOPLE ARE DISCOVERING
SOMETHING WONDERFUL. *THEIR HERITAGE.*

Arcadia Publishing is the leading local history publisher in the United States. With more than 4,000 titles in print and hundreds of new titles released every year, Arcadia has extensive specialized experience chronicling the history of communities and celebrating America's hidden stories, bringing to life the people, places, and events from the past. To discover the history of other communities across the nation, please visit:

www.arcadiapublishing.com

Customized search tools allow you to find regional history books about the town where you grew up, the cities where your friends and family live, the town where your parents met, or even that retirement spot you've been dreaming about.

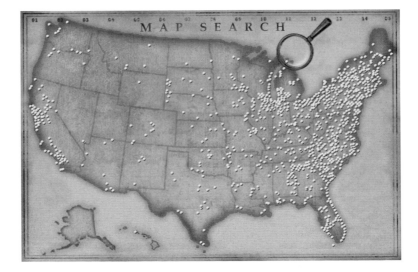